Dear Girlfriends Forever! Love, Jane

WE WENT SHOPPING · WE KEPT SECRETS · WE PLAYED HOPSCOTCH · WE LAY

IN THE SUN · WE WENT DANCING · WE HAD TEA · WE WORE MINI SKIRTS · WE SANG IN THE CAR · WE ATE

WE LAUGHED SOOOOO HARD ·

· WE LIP SYNCED · WE WENT TO PARIS · WE WENT TO HATS · WE TRIED ON LUNCH

FRENCH FRIES · WE BORROWED CLOTHES · WE CRUISED FOR GUYS · WE WENT TO

in Tickle-Me Pink

We are not
interested
in the
possibilities
of defeat.
♥ Queen Victoria

A N D   M E ♥

The laughter of girls is, & ever was among the delightful sounds of the earth. ♥ De Quincey

GIRLFRIENDS

Girlfriends Forever

from the
HEART of the HOME

OUR GREATEST VICTORY IS NOT IN NEVER FALLING, BUT IN RISING EVERY TIME WE FALL. ♥ CONFUCIUS

Susan Branch

Little, Brown and Company
Boston · New York · London

Copyright © 2000 by  Susan Stewart Branch

ALL RIGHTS RESERVED

No part of this book may be reproduced in any form or by any electronic or mechanical means, including information storage and retrieval systems, without permission in writing from the publisher, except by a reviewer who may quote brief passages in a review.
Second Printing
ISBN 0-316-10623-2

Excerpts from Mostly True by Brian Andreas. Copyright © 1993 by Brian Andreas. Reprinted by permission of Brian Andreas. ❤

Excerpt from "Pooh Goes Visiting & Gets Into a Tight Place" by A.A. Milne, from WINNIE-THE-POOH by A.A. Milne, copyright 1926 by E.P. Dutton, renewed 1954 by A.A. Milne. Used by permission of Dutton Children's Books, a division of Penguin Putnam Inc. ❤

RRD-IN

PRINTED IN THE
UNITED STATES OF AMERICA

My 11 year old nieces Holly & Heidi might not think they have too much in common with these bathing beauties. But they'd be wrong. That is their great grandma (on the left) with her best friends, playing just the way my nieces do, & the tie that binds is their hopes & dreams. ♥

This book is dedicated to the things that connect women, past, present & future: courage, energy, nurturing spirit, & heart; their dedication to home & family. ♥ It's for sisters, grandmas, aunts, moms & daughters — & for the best friends we couldn't live without. ♥

A candle passes its fire from wick to wick & loses nothing in the act.

LAVERNE & SHIRLEY · LUCY

·LOUISE· & ·ETHEL· OPRAH & GAIL·

ALONE WE CAN DO SO LITTLE
TOGETHER WE CAN DO SO MUCH

It's a Party!

TIARAS OPTIONAL

THELMA &

·BETTY & VERONICA·

CONTENTS

INTIMACIES BETWEEN WOMEN OFTEN GO BACKWARDS, BEGINNING IN REVELATION AND ENDING UP IN SMALL TALK WITHOUT LOSS OF ESTEEM. ❧ ELIZABETH BOWEN ❧

Oh, the comfort—the inexpressible comfort of feeling *safe* with a person— having neither to weigh thoughts nor measure words, but pouring them all right out, just as they are, chaff & grain together; certain that a faithful hand will take & sift them, keep what is worth keeping, & then with the breath of kindness, *blow* the rest away.

♥ *Dinah Maria Mulock Craik* (1866)

What do women talk about? Women's conversation starts in the middle, goes to the beginning, & doesn't have an end. We stop talking as we part & pick up right where we left off when we meet again. What do we talk about? Big things & little things: world peace, children, food, art, money, love, work, spirituality, movies & men, for starters. So that's how this book works — no beginning, no end, you can start in the middle & work from the inside out if you like. It goes from chocolate to heartbreak to boyfriends & back again. Talking to our girlfriends cheers us up & makes us feel connected. This book is here to help you fight off the "lonelies" when there are no girlfriends around — which, hopefully (thankfully) is rare. ♥

NEED I SAY MORE?

There were two ducks; the female with the brown head & the other with the green head ~ the unfemale.
♥ DANIELLE RETTINGER – AGE 5

MOTIVATION

ME

I'm a girlfriend's girlfriend. ♥ I come by it naturally because I grew up in a totally macho, Pop Warner, Three Stooges kind of world. Spiders in the face, snakes on the kitchen table, rough housing, slingshots, BB guns, motorcycles & fried baloney sandwiches were normal. I'm the oldest of 8 children; first me, then my 4 brothers & then (finally!) my 3 sisters. For the first 10 years it was me & Mom ~ & THEM. My mom was my 1st best friend; girlfriends were really important to me from the beginning. When I was 6, we were the first family to move onto a street of new houses ~ for a while it seemed like no best friend would EVER move in. Finally, one day I found a little girl's baby buggy in a yard down the street. YAY! It was like finding a steaming hot bowl of chicken soup on the moon ~ I found a kindred spirit. ♥

US CAMPING

THEY'RE GOOD LOOKIN' & THEY SEEM INNOCENT, BUT DO NOT BE DECEIVED. ♥ (THEY DROVE MY MOM & SISTERS TO THIS!)

BUT NO – WE WOULDN'T TRADE THEM FOR THE WORLD ☺.

*L*ater, all the best friends I could hope for moved into the neighborhood & there were years & years of hide-'n'-seek, lemonade stands, shows & circuses, rollerskating, jacks, "house," dolls, & hopscotch. Our house seemed to be the center of the earth. The whole neighborhood gathered there, boys and girls. For one thing, we had a swimming pool, & for another thing, we had a wonderful mother ♥. Because of the teasing, the ear-piercing screams, the whining of dripping-wet children telling on each other at her screen door, she divided, & conquered: Girls Day and Boys Day at the Pool. So my friends & I could play "Mermaid" in peace, without a "King of the Mountain" drowning us in belly-flop water. ♥

US

THEM

MORE THEM

When women are depressed they either eat or go shopping. Men invade another country. It's a whole different way of thinking. ♥ ELAYNE BOOSLER

-11-

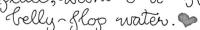

(left margin, bottom to top): DOWN BY THE SEASHORE ♥ DOWN BY THE SEA ♥ JOHNNY BROKE A BOTTLE AND BLAMED IT

(right margin, top to bottom): SO HA! HA! HA! HOW MANY LICKINS DID JOHNNY GET? ONE! TWO! THREE! FOUR! FIVE!

We were Just Seventeen
(You know what I mean)

Karen Bennett was there for "Girls Day at the Pool" & she was my best friend all through high school. She's the one who found out about French Kissing & told me walking home from school. We taught each other to dance (practicing the bop with the refrigerator door handle), were on the drill team together, made pom poms at a slumber party, double dated to the drive-in, ran amok in Lake Arrowhead & bonded for life, forever. ♥

Our most "famous" escapade is that (GET READY) we . . . MET THE BEATLES! YES! ♥ After their first concert at the Hollywood Bowl, on a tip extracted from an overwhelmed cab driver, we stalked them in to Bel Air (stopping first at a gas station to make ourselves beautiful – just in case). There were 4 or 5 cars out front when we found the house, too many for us, so we parked a couple of streets away & began to reconnoiter the neighborhood. Whispering our plan, we went through backyards in unfamiliar territory arriving just in time (about midnight) to see them (the boys) get out of the pool & run to the house in the moonlight in their little tiny English bathing suits. After a few minutes we followed them up to the wide porch where we could hear piano playing & singing & laughing, but couldn't see anything because the curtains were pulled. We had a perfect view of the staircase, however,

& as we stood there trying to figure out what to do next ~ John came bounding down the stairs ~ in his underwear (Jockeys). Karen saw him first & threw herself against a wall ~ I was behind her, didn't see him coming & suddenly we were eyeball to eyeball! Very soon a manager came out, scraped us off the floor ~ & suggested we "come back tomorrow." (Like this was easy.)

It took a full day of begging phone calls to my Dad's work the next day before he finally let me have the car. By this time the whole world knew they were there ~ "no parking" signs were everywhere & it was a teenage mob scene. But we had the lay of the land from the night before. Nonchalantly, we strolled past the Bel Air Police, got ourselves into a backyard & we were home free ~ up past the pool & there they all stood on the porch! John flapped his elbows at us & barked (despite our special beauty stop, he didn't seem to remember us from the night before), Ringo flashed his rings, Paul was adorable & George seemed shy.

THE BEATLES

All those years ago...

We got their autographs & hid them under our clothes as we boldly walked past the police ~ discovering the police were as excited as we were, wanting to hear about everything! We sang "I'll Follow the Sun," "Baby's in Black," "She Loves You" Yeah Yeah Yeah all the way home, our dream fulfilled, our lives blessed. Karen was the perfect person to be 17 with ~ we can still laugh till we cry. She was there for my 50th birthday & we danced the bop. ♥

Karen is the reason most of the people in my art have beautiful red hair. ♥

Watercolor Memories of

WHEN JUPITER ALIGNS WITH MARS
THEN PEACE WILL GUIDE THE PLANETS

the Way we Were . . .

Floppy Hat w/ Sunflower

Granny Glasses

LOLITA

♪ It was an itsy-bitsy teeny-weeny yellow ♪ Polka-dot bikini

Flower Power

White Lipstick

Crop top

Love Beads

Hip-Hugger Bell-Bottoms

Peace & love

Leather Shoulder-Bag with Fringe

Can you dig it?

Platform shoes for dancing till dawn

You only live once, but if you work it right, once is enough. ♥

Go-Go Boots

14

SUE & JANET

Janet & Sue

I graduated from high school before Karen & moved into an apartment with my other best friend Janet Campbell. For 3 glorious fun-filled years, we lived the quintessential teenage-girls-in-an-apartment-of-their-own lifestyle. We were legends in our own minds: Lucy & Ethel, Laverne & Shirley, Janet & Sue. We cleaned house at midnight; did laundry at 2am, slept till noon, lay by the pool all day & ate Taco Bell only — we celebrated freedom from parents! We put on make up together, usually ending up making such funny faces that we would cry off whatever we put on, laughing. We flew our 1st airplane flight EVER together in a plane ominously (we thought) named "The Silver Dart"; danced "The Jerk" at The Yum Yum Tree in white vinyl miniskirts; & dyed Janet's hair whatever was the color of the heroine's in the movie (Ann Margaret's color worked best) we saw at the drive-in. We tried false eyelashes, push-up bras, Blue Nun, & Janis Joplin.

When you come right down to it, the secret of having it all is believing that you do ♥

ON THE ROAD AGAIN

JANET WAS JUANA, JUANITA, JAN, JANNIE, YAN, YANNIE & Natasha

VALLEY GIRLS

We loved the Beatles but the Rolling Stones kind of scared us. When we moved into our new apartment, rather than let anyone (cute-boy neighbors) see us in our waitress uniforms, we climbed out our kitchen window & snuck to the car. Janet's boyfriend, Jim Haley (who she's still married to ♥→) went to Viet Nam & gave her his little black MG Midget convertible sportscar to drive. One day the soft top ripped — instead of buying a new one (expensive), we bought matching hats & blankets. We drove everywhere, wind in our faces, radio up, us singing ♫ SHE'S GOT AN E-GYPTIAN RING THAT SPARKLES BEFORE SHE SPEAKS ♫ — gas was 25¢ a gallon — we could go around the world on that! We weren't hippies, didn't sit in, didn't know there WAS a Woodstock till the movie came out — we spent most of our time dancing, flirting, shopping or crying over old movies. Just old-fashioned girls ☺. Money, since we didn't have any, was no object & although we always supported ourselves, no job was worth the sacrifice of an adventure, & EVERYTHING

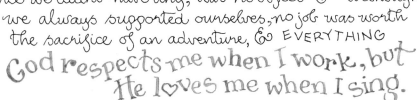
God respects me when I work, but He loves me when I sing.

RABINDRANATH TAGORE

TARZAN & ME

THAT IS A CHEETAH

FERNANDITO CHULO, BABY LIONS, & ME.

was an adventure. It was a way of saying we didn't have turns out to be a good thing. lived to tell the stories. ♥

LA-DEE-DA?

LA-DEE-DA INDEED!

simpler time, which is another a thought in our heads. Which It made us brave PLUS we

From our spur-of-the-moment trip to Mexico City (went for the weekend, stayed a month) to visit my boyfriend, the wild-animal trainer for the Tarzan T.V. Show, to the time we came home from the beach to find that Janet's dog had torn our entire trash into teeny bits & that our apt. looked like there'd been a ticker-tape parade in it, not to mention that we'd "forgotten" to wash dishes for a week, & we'd invited people to stop in on their way home ~ EVERYTHING was FUN and NEW to us ♥

At the end, we knew in our hearts our time was almost up & we tried to run; when Tim came home from Viet Nam, there were price tags on all our furniture ~ we were moving to Hawaii! We never stood a chance. Tim (THE GUY WHO CAME OUT ONCE DRESSED IN JANET'S FURRY PINK BUNNY JAMMIES, UNSHAVEN, CARRYING A BEER ☺) had other ideas, & he had first dibs ~ he & Janet had been in love since they were 15! Janet was IT for him & still is. He stole her away so they could live happily ever after. I have forgiven him ♥ (but just barely ☺). Now their two daughters know our stories almost better than we do! And the beat goes on. ♥

Constant use had not run ragged the fabric of their friendship.

♥ DOROTHY PARKER

YOUTH IS JUST A MOMENT ~ BUT IT IS A MOMENT YOU CARRY FOREVER IN YOUR HEART. ♥

Who's in Charge Here?

When we were young it was easy to know who the adults were — they were the people over 30. ♥ They were the people we weren't supposed to trust — now we ARE them. (How can this be?)

How do you know you're an adult? If my friends are adults, does that mean I'm one too? My friends are tall — they drink coffee & drive cars. But they also

Buon Giorno Principesse!

hide chocolate in their underwear drawers, eat ice cream straight from the container, still like someone to tell them a story, & enjoy playing outside. ♥ Maybe no one ever really grows up. Maybe we just get to be older & older kids. Maybe the whole world is being run by old kids. ♥

♥ AFTER ADAIR LARA

Are you a princess? I said & she said I'm much more than a princess but you don't have a name for it yet here on earth. ♥ Brian Andreas

LOVE

CAROLYN MILLS

I was 21 years old & I was on my way to a job interview. I dressed carefully, tied a ribbon around my ankle, put a flower in my hair (it was the 70's!) & off I went.

In the middle of the interview, I fell in love. And of course, for all the right reasons.

The young man (my future "boss") had broken his shoulder; his arm was in a sling held together with two Velcro strips. As he was trying to write on my application I saw a look of frustration cross his face, his sling was slowing down his writing hand. Rip—Riiip, APART came the Velcro, OFF went the sling & Zing! went the strings of my heart. Who could resist THAT? I was putty.

There you have it — #23 of "THE GOOD & INTELLIGENT REASONS TO FALL IN LOVE"— Velcro-ripping noises.

The very first time I fell in love I was 6 & I loved him because of his red cowboy shirt. At 12, the object of my affections qualified because he had a silver tooth. I was maturing. From Velcro-ripping noises I went on to English accents & guys who loved French music. Today, only a few of the many reasons I love Joe is that he loves trains, Christmas, cooking, & ME! (Not necessarily in that order.) ♥

So much as she loves his love of her; Then

loves she her lover. For love of her

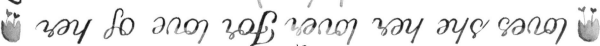

lover, Or love of her love of her lover?

WOMEN'S TEARS

Delicious tears! the heart's own dew. ❤ *L. E. Landon*

       What is it about us & crying? Love can make us cry but it doesn't even take that much! I cry almost every day. I look for movies that will make me cry. I don't consider myself <u>especially</u> sappy but I never got through one single episode of <u>Little House on the Prairie</u> without crying (that Pa!). The news makes me cry ~ commercials make me cry. I cry when Rosie O'Donnell gives away a trip to Disney World. When the U.S. Women's Soccer Team won, I was glued to the T.V., crying. If I come in on the last 5 min. of a sad movie, I cry as if I'd watched the whole thing. I can't watch animal movies anymore ~ <u>Old Yeller</u> almost did me in & since then I can't bear to watch any escaping dolphins or hitchhiking, country-crossing, limping cats & dogs. I cry when Frank Sinatra sings "Polka Dots & Moonbeams" ~ & when Audrey Hepburn cut her hair in <u>Roman Holiday</u> (because it was so <u>unbearably adorable</u>). I thought I would die when Melly Wilkes died in <u>Gone With the Wind</u> ~ I missed dinner that night (I was 14 & just starting out on my long career in tears).

       Needless to say, with my best friends, the tears have run the gamut ~ we cry for beauty, for love, for heart, for sad, for courage, for fun & because we can't help it. ❤

She said she usually cried at least once a day not because she was sad but because the world was so beautiful & life was so short. ❤ BRIAN ANDREAS

IF YOU'RE HAPPY & YOU KNOW IT, CLAP YOUR HANDS.

HER LITTLE GIRL WAS LATE ARRIVING HOME FROM SCHOOL SO THE MOTHER BEGAN TO SCOLD HER, BUT STOPPED & ASKED, "WHY ARE YOU SO LATE?" "I HAD TO HELP ANOTHER GIRL. SHE WAS IN TROUBLE," REPLIED THE DAUGHTER.

"WHAT DID YOU DO TO HELP HER?"

"OH, I sat down & HELPED HER CRY."

GIRL TALK

THE BEST WAY TO MEND A BROKEN HEART IS TIME & GIRLFRIENDS. ♥ GWYNETH PALTROW

There I was, out on the open highway — windows down, breezes blowing, Patsy Cline on the radio, going about 70 mph on a gorgeous day — everything perfect. All of a sudden, out of nowhere, a big cement wall appeared & I slammed into it going full blast.... I lay there in a heap for 2 years; then I got up, crawled into the smashed car, turned it around & limped back down the road doing a cool ½ mph, a mere shadow of my formerly fabulous self. ♥

That's what it felt like 2 years after my marriage ended, when I awoke to find that I had moved myself lock, stock, & barrel 3,000 miles away from everything & everybody I'd known & loved to an island off the coast of Massachusetts where they had this thing called WINTER. Apparently I had attempted to escape heartbreak, but it wasn't working. I could barely stand to look at myself in the mirror — I had NO idea who I was or what I wanted. It was clear a new dress or even a new boyfriend was not going to bring me out of this — I had to get radical. On the next few pages, with the help of wise words from world sages, I'll tell you what I learned in case You ever get in a "car wreck" like mine. ♥
('Cause that's what friends are for. ♥)

THE VERY MOST IMPORTANT THING I LEARNED IS THIS:

Seek not outside yourself — Heaven is within.
♥ Mary Lou Cook

TRUE "POWER"
(GIRL OR OTHERWISE)
Comes from Inside

Everyone knows about the little voice inside us all that "seldom leads us wrong & never into folly." We are encouraged to listen to it, we call it intuition or the voice of our better selves — our conscience. I think that's what brought me to Martha's Vineyard — I know it's what kept me here. ❤

THE AWAKENING OF CONSCIOUSNESS IS NOT UNLIKE THE CROSSING OF A FRONTIER—ONE STEP AND YOU ARE IN ANOTHER COUNTRY. ❤ADRIENNE RICH

But there's this OTHER VOICE — the LOUDER one. The one that NEVER SHUTS UP. It's never happy about anything & it lies. The second my eyes open in the morning, there it is, crouching, ready to leap at me to tell me everything I didn't accomplish yesterday & what I won't get done today. After it sees me in the mirror, I get a quick lecture on how fat I am & how hideous my hair is. So far, I haven't been able to **KILL** it, but I'm trying. Until then, I try to remember that this voice is inside ME — I'm the one in charge, not it. I've got that voice in a training camp now — it's perfectly capable of recognizing & reminding me of my good qualities, & why shouldn't it? I feel so much better when it does! Our thoughts really do create our reality. ❤

Everything, all joy, all happiness, all sadness comes from inside. You may think chocolate will help you feel better, or a new dress or car or diamond ring (& there is something to be said for those things) but for the long run it's like putting a Bandaid on a gunshot wound. It will never be enough. Without inner fulfillment those things only make us feel more empty.

> The only people who never fail are those who never try.
> ❤ ILKA CHASE

IF YOU CAN DREAM IT

YOU CAN MAKE IT SO.

CONSCIOUS THINKING

When my mother was little she visited her grandma (on her farm in Iowa) & saw a piece of paper with dining room furniture cut out from a magazine & glued on to it. Her grandma explained that this was exactly what she had in mind for her dining room. She said she had cut it out so she could look at it every day & "think on it."

The power of conscious thinking has been around for a long time ~even longer than my great-grandma! I like to think it came out of that great well of information & inspiration they call "old wives' tales." The first book to explain the

power of conscious thinking was written in 1937 by Napoleon Hill & called _Think & Grow Rich_ (and he wasn't just talking about money). He asked the big question: "If you can't control what goes on in your own mind, how can you hope to guide your destiny?"

Hundreds of wonderful books, written since _Think & Grow Rich_, have embellished fully on this theme. They're changing the world & they're all out there for the taking & learning. I've loved these: _Anatomy of the Spirit_ (Myss), _The Road Less Traveled_ (Peck), _The 7 Spiritual Laws of Success_ (Chopra), _The Power of Unconditional Love_ (Keyes)~ There are so many good ones! Oh! & for creative inspiration, _The Artist's Way_ (Cameron & Bryan).

The centre that I cannot find
is known to my unconscious mind.
I have no reason to despair
because I am already there.

W. H. Auden

SOMETIMES THE WAY TO BE IN TOUCH WITH THE WORLD IS TO BE OUT OF TOUCH. ♥

Coming Home

> We need time to dream, time to remember, time to reach for the infinite. Time to be.
> GLADYS TABER

In *The Wizard of Oz*, Dorothy always had the power to go home in her ruby slippers—she just didn't know it. All of us have the power to go "home" too—home to our center where peace, faith & spirit reside. There are probably 100 ways to get there, all of them good, & everyone must find their own way (TOO BAD WE CAN'T GET OUR HANDS ON THOSE SHOES! ☺).

For me the way home was through meditation. I took a course & learned how. And when I got there it was as safe & secure as my mother's embrace & I found faith like a shining-star-gift-from-God waiting for me. ♥ It had ALWAYS been there, I just didn't know it. It was in the QUIET that I could see it. ♥

FINDING YOUR DREAMS

ALL MY LIFE I'VE BEEN CIRCLING & CIRCLING THE TOWER OF THE LORD & I STILL DON'T KNOW IF I'M A POET, A STORM, OR A SONG. ♥

When I came to Martha's Vineyard I had NO idea what my dreams even were. It was much easier for me to recite what I didn't like about my life. So here's a little exercise I learned that helped me get a handle on it: make a list of 12 things you love about your life, i.e. "my cats," "my energy," "my friends," etc. Set it aside. Now make a list of 12 things you don't like: "my job," "my car," "my weight," etc. Now change those dislikes to positive choices: "I choose to change jobs," "I choose to have a new car," "I choose to lose weight."

Voila! Now you know what you want! The next step is to practice the conscious thinking that will help those choices become reality. →

25

The Secret of Success is Constancy of Purpose.
♥Disraeli

Close your eyes, take a deep breath & relax. Picture yourself re- ceiving your choice (i.e. making your dream come true). See yourself in that picture. Notice how it feels to have it; what you think about it. See every detail. Do this every day & soon it will permeate from your conscious thinking to your unconscious power center. Affirmations such as this are a big help. The hardest part for me was doing this every day (& I still DON'T! Don't confuse me with one of those perfect people!) but the discipline of the course I took really helped — now I can get there anytime I want to even if its not every day. ♥   I think TRYING counts.♥

Louisa May Alcott wrote:

I do not ask for any crown but that
which all may win;
Nor try to conquer any world,
except the one within.
Be Thou my guide until I find, led by
a tender hand,
The happy kingdom in myself & dare
to take command. ♥

GIRL POWER

Neglect not
the gift
that is in
thee...
1 Timothy 4:14

♪ LET'S GET TOGETHER, Yeah - Yeah - Yeah ♪

It's been going on forever & it starts when we're young— from our first birthday parties to Girl Scout camping trips, slumber parties, & baby showers — reasons to "get together" abound. And when there isn't a reason, we make one up! ♥

NINE TODAY ♥

"Tuesday Girls" was at my house in California every Tuesday afternoon. The idea was for us to teach each other things. For months, Liz taught us quilting. While we talked & laughed we made wonderful things. Later, Janet taught us to make fabric-covered, heart-shaped, padded picture frames. I gave a few art lessons & also a noodle-making class that included lunch with wine (the beginning of the end). Then it was Diana's turn (we knew this would be good). She told us to bring our bathing suits (what? mermaid? water ballet??). The next week she came with a blender, turned up the music & taught us how to make margaritas! Then we lay by the pool all afternoon. What a rousing success Diana's Day turned out to be. From then on it was always Diana's Day on Tuesday. Why didn't we think of that?

TUESDAY GIRLS GO CHRISTMAS CAROLING (BUT FIRST — FOCUS!)

DIANA WITH FRUITS OF LABOR

Well-behaved women rarely make history.

♥ LAUREL THATCHER ULRICH

I've given & gone to lots of Girl Parties & they're always fun.
Margot's birthday lunch was the "pink of perfection" — even the food was pink!
It started with pink "Skip & Go
Nakeds" served in antique sherry
glasses, then....

MENU

Cold Raspberry Soup
with ice cream "croutons"

Grilled Salmon with Orange
Sauce & Pink Peppercorns

Tinted Quinoa with
POMEGRANATE SEEDS

Heart-shaped PINK Crostini

Strawberry Shortcake
And
C H O C O L A T E S
(WHICH NO ONE CARED
IF THEY WERE
PINK OR NOT :)

Maybe the
greatest Girl Party
I ever gave was a Basket Party/Wine Tasting. (Only one photo has
survived from that night & it barely begins to tell
the story ❤.) A Basket Party works on the same
premise as a Tupperware Party only there are beautiful baskets for sale. A nearby winery had provided
us with a wine sampler (a big one!). My diary counts
30 guests, but notes that "friends brought friends."
I'd made lots of taste treats including stuffed French Bread &
Chocolate Eclairs. There was brilliant conversation (of course), music &
laughter. It was so much fun that after the basket presentation, the
music was cranked & dancing broke out all over — lasting till
after midnight (my diary says I went to bed at 2:30am!). To top it off,
everybody bought so many baskets that I got one of those big
basket trunks with the brass hinges FREE — my "hostess gift" — I
almost felt guilty (all this & furniture too!). ❤

P A R T Y   G I R L S

Hearts that never lean, must fall.
♥ Emily Dickinson

My mom plays Jacks with her tennis girlfriends. ♥

Girlfriends aren't a luxury (though they sure feel like one!). They are a healthy necessity. Women process through talking. We're all busier these days, but it's been proven that women who lack the social support of other women are more susceptible to illness — that's why those girls are so healthy! ♥

T G I F

Besides our regular TGIF's at each other's houses, we meet to admire each other's gardens, look at each other's new wallpaper, bring each other soup, celebrate each other's accomplishments & dry each other's tears. Last week, I woke Margot at 5:30 am & we went on a drive, windows down, music playing, while most of the island still slept; got coffee, looked at gardens & caught up. ♥

The TGIF Girls have already decided ~ when we're old, we want to have the "Hippy Hippy Shake Retirement Home" & live together, fat & happily ever after. ♥

P.S. You might not know it, but we had some pretty good "Boy Parties" too. ♥

AIN'T LIFE GRAND?

30

On the road between the
houses of friends
grass does not grow. ♥

LONG LASTING FRIENDSHIPS

Flower for a lifetime

TRUE BLUE

LOYAL

Supportive

Smart

COMMUNICATIVE

Funny

CULTIVATE YOUR GARDEN

WITH

LOVE

♫ Still crazy

After all these years ♪

FOREVER ♥ FRIENDS

A best friend can last your whole life, so when you're old you'll have someone who shares your memories & knew you "when" — then the laughter never has to end. They're easiest to come by when you're young, so if you're 10 & reading this (Hi! ♥), get all the best friends you can & never lose them. Here are some ideas on where to find new friends: Get involved with something that meets regularly & for a long time, so friendship has a chance to develop. Join a book club 📖, or an investment club, sewing or craft classes, creative writing classes, a meditation group, yoga class, or exercise group. You can volunteer to support a candidate, be a Big Sister, put together a fund raiser, be a Girl Scout leader, or join the Junior League. To keep a best friend you have to be nice, be loyal, & be forgiving. To have a best friend you must BE a best friend. To be loved, you must be loveable ♥. The rewards? Support, solace, fun, encouragement, comfort, trust, adventure, love, & laughter.

YES'M, OLD FRIENDS IS ALWAYS BEST, 'LESS YOU CAN CATCH A NEW ONE THAT'S FIT TO MAKE AN OLD ONE OUT OF. ♥ SARAH ORNE JEWETT

-33-

♪ Caring, Sharing,
Every Little Thing that We
are Wearing... ♪

SISTERS

DOROTHY PARKER• HELEN KELLER• LOUISA MAY ALCOTT

LUCILLE BALL• GEORGIA O'KEEFFE•FLORENCE GRIFFITH JOYNER

Nothing great was ever achieved without Enthusiasm.

Ralph Waldo Emerson

CYNICISM

KILL IT BEFORE IT MULTIPLIES

ELEANOR ROOSEVELT • ALICE WALKER ♥

You one it, I two it, you three it, I four it, you five it, I six it, you seven it, I jumped over it, and you eight it...

WORDS

Ten measures of speech descended on the world; women took nine & men one. ♥ BABYLONIAN TALMUD

Oh yeah, we can talk. Women know the power of words — we solve all our problems through language.

We know the wrong word at the wrong time can end a friendship, wound a soul, bring tears. Just the right words can heal, lift up, create joy — make us laugh till we cry, and connect our lives. ♥

I don't remember saying "bad" words when I was young, but I must have brought home something my mom didn't like because I remember her telling me that I didn't have to use the same words as everybody else — she said I could make up my own words — TRA-LA! This was very exciting to me — I wasted no time getting →

CAN WE TALK?

started. Today my sisters (& many of my friends) & I talk a language all our own. From "nurking" (which means puttering around) to "crunchy" (achy from sleeping wrong) — to "death on a stick" (something really boring) & "international invitation" (when someone overlooks the obvious: "what do you need, an international invitation?"). If we love you, you are "Little Sportheart," "Bo-Bo," "Pokey Man," "Mr. Mo Mo," or "Poon Dog." We redefined some words — for instance "You throw like a girl" means "great throw, good arm, nice shoulder muscles, good eye." "You run like a girl" means "what style! marathon material!" "You cry like a girl" means "your compassion & humanity are clearly visible & one of my favorite things about you." ♥   Words can lift us up—

God sent His singers upon the earth, with songs of sadness & of mirth, that they might touch the hearts of men, & bring them back to heaven again. Henry Wadsworth Longfellow

Besides us :· — there are true wordmeisters — people who make music from a string of graceful words. Everything that even mattered has been beautifully said by someone whose attestment has teeth.

For instance, Helen Keller (famous American woman who was rendered blind & deaf in her infancy, HAD NO VOICE until she was 7, & then gave us words back as pearls) said, "I seldom think of my limitations & they never make me sad. Perhaps there is just a touch of yearning at times, but it is vague, like a breeze among flowers."

↳ BREEZE AMONG FLOWERS

Anne Frank, who hid from the Nazis for 2 years then died in a camp at age 15, wrote, "IN SPITE OF EVERYTHING I STILL BELIEVE THAT PEOPLE ARE REALLY GOOD AT HEART. ♥"

WORDS LOVE, HEAL, GIVE HOPE.

BOOKS

When I give a favorite book to a friend I give, not strings of beautiful words, but acres & acres. I get a thrill when I think of them enjoying something I love so much ~ it's like giving the gift of a vacation to a whole new place. ♥

Whenever my friends & I get together we always exchange "book notes" ~ who's reading what ~ what's good. I don't keep every book I read because some of them don't deserve it ~ but I make sure I keep the ones I love.

FROM MY SHELF OF FOREVER-LOVED "CLASSICS"

Mists of Avalon
Excellent Women
Enchanted April
Marjorie Morningstar
A Woman of Independent Means
Atlas Shrugged
My Brilliant Career

West with the Night
Portrait of a Marriage
Charms for the Easy Life
Autobiography of Mark Twain
Abigail Adams
9 Steps to Financial Freedom
The Rules

I collect old children's picture books; I have a shelf of books written by & about my heroes (I'm hoping their spirits osmosis themselves into me!), & I also have old copies of all my childhood favorites, <u>Pollyanna</u> (the "Glad" book), <u>Little Women</u> ~ these books are all in my studio where I work every day so I'm surrounded by inspiration & genius. I need all the help I can get ♥!

CHICK FLICKS ROCK

"Let me not be sad because I am born a woman
In this world; many saints suffer in this way."
♥ Janabai (c. 1340)

The Academy Awards happened last Sunday & "Shakespeare in Love" won for Best Picture. I loved that movie—I've actually seen it in the theatre 3 times (so far!). The last time was yesterday (afternoon matinee).

I took my brilliant, gorgeous artist girlfriend Margot so I could live vicariously through her appreciative eyes seeing it for the first time ♥. We both just cried from the beauty of it all. Have you seen it? You'll love it!

I was raised on Shirley Temple & Fred Astaire/Ginger Rogers movies. They brought me never-ending joy & turned me into a person who TOTALLY believes in fairy tales. What a world of inspiration movies can be! If you want to see romance, clothes, furniture, architecture & dancing to make you cry from loveliness (not to mention heavenly music) see Rogers & Astaire in "Carefree." Another movie with wonderful rooms with romantic wallpaper & curtains is "Dear Ruth" with Wm. Holden. "Love Letters" with Jos. Cotten & Jennifer Jones has darling English cottages & gardens. "The Women" has great houses & hats (but very creepy women!). For story see "Shirley Valentine," "Somewhere in Time," two Barbara Stanwycks: "Ball of Fire" & "The Lady Eve," "Anne of Green Gables," ♥ "Bachelor Mother" (Rogers & Niven) & for a rainy day "Enchanted Cottage."

ONE OF THE SECRETS OF A HAPPY LIFE IS
CONTINUOUS SMALL TREATS. ♥ Iris Murdoch

IT'S THE LITTLE THINGS
THAT MEAN THE MOST

Winning-the-lottery type
happiness is short-lived ~
even a trip to Disney World or a
new car won't do it for the long term. It's the little
things in life: play with your cat, plant a
garden, take your kids to the park, bake a
pie, take time to be a friend. ♥ Keep putting
the little moments together & they'll turn to

CONTENTMENT

TRUTH

LITTLE DROPS OF WATER,
LITTLE GRAINS OF SAND,
MAKE THE MIGHTY OCEAN
AND THE PLEASANT LAND.
THUS THE LITTLE MINUTES,
Humble though they be,
MAKE THE MIGHTY AGES
of eternity. ~ ♥ Julia A. Fletcher

Never underestimate the value

of the little moment ♥.

NEVER LIVE FASTER THAN YOUR GUARDIAN ANGELS CAN FLY

KIND WORDS

GOOD BOOKS

The modern rule is that every woman must be her own chaperone. ♥ Amy Vanderbilt

It's a toxic world but YOU HAVE THE POWER to protect yourself. ♥ Feed your life from the well of SWEETNESS.

MUSIC THAT MAKES YOUR SPIRIT SOAR

MOVIES THAT INSPIRE

Everybody gets so much information all day long that they lose their common sense. ♥ Gertrude Stein

TAKING GOOD CARE

STRESS ✿ RELIEF

BE YOUR OWN BEST FRIEND

No day is so bad
it can't be fixed
with a nap. *Carrie Snow*

THE CHALLENGE

SOLUTIONS

It's been proven that STRESS causes actual changes to the immune system. YIKES!

It's caused by almost everything ~ divorce and death; normal life pressures, fears, too much T.V. news ~ even happy things like Christmas, outstanding personal achievement, or building a house.

If it goes on too long it steals vitality and causes illness. It's cumulative and it sneaks up on you ~ especially when you are too busy to notice!

Exercise and meditation strengthen stamina. Daily doses keep you ready in case of sudden life changes.

Bubble baths, massage, being with friends, deep breathing, healthy diet, hobbies & fun refresh the spirit.

Laughter builds up the immune system (get hooked on funny books & comedies).

Learn to say NO!

Talking through problems with a professional is sooo helpful ~ getting problems out of the dark & into the light makes them less scary. ♥

Love the one you're with

Keep rosemary by your garden gate. Add pepper to your mashed potatoes. Plant roses & lavender for luck. Fall in love whenever you can.
♥ *Alice Hoffman*

How to be Happy

FEED the BIRDS

EAT GOOD FOOD

Take Long Walks

BREATHE FRESH AIR

Wear Something Pretty

Read Good Books

GROW FLOWERS

redecorate (p.57)

TAKE LONG NAPS

Soak in Bathtubs

Write in a Diary

SHOW LOVE

Paint Toenails

SEE CHICK FLICKS

FUN WITH CLOTHES

CLOTHES MAKE THE MAN. NAKED PEOPLE HAVE LITTLE OR NO INFLUENCE IN SOCIETY.

MARK TWAIN

How we put ourselves together can be very revealing as to what kind of person we are. Here are a few little things you can do with your clothes to make the whole process more interesting & at the same time express your joie de vivre, confidence & energy, you 100% original thing, you! ♥

TWIST A LONG SCARF THROUGH BELT LOOPS ON BAGGY PANTS (ESPECIALLY LINEN PANTS) À LA FRED ASTAIRE ♥.

DOUBLE OPERA-LENGTH PEARLS OR BEADS AROUND YOUR NECK & HOOK TOGETHER WITH A LARGE BROOCH.

ANKLE RIBBON

TIE A PRETTY PIECE OF RIBBON (FRENCH OR OTHERWISE) ROUND & ROUND & ROUND YOUR WRIST; TUCK IN ENDS OR LEAVE THEM OUT. WEAR IT PLAIN, WITH A BRACELET, OR PIN A BROOCH ONTO IT. ♥

MY SISTER MARY LOOKS ADORABLE IN SHORT DRESSES OVER PANTS. ♥

ALWAYS ALWAYS ALWAYS WEAR TOENAIL POLISH IN THE SUMMER (ONE COAT PRACTICALLY LASTS ALL SUMMER!). TOE RINGS CAN BE CUTE (THUMB RINGS TOO) & PAINTING EACH NAIL A DIFFERENT COLOR IS FUN FOR THE BEACH. ♥

I base my fashion taste on what doesn't itch. ♥ *Gilda Radner*

FANCY PANTS

FOR JEANS, EMBROIDER FLOWERS OR BUTTERFLIES ON POCKETS & HEMS. ADD FABRIC BORDER TO HEMS. FOR CAPRIS: CUT OFF HEMS OF BLACK PANTS, TRIM W/ LACE OR FRINGE ~ JEWEL TRIM ~ RHINESTONE TEARDROPS! GET TRIMS AT FABRIC OR CRAFT STORES. SPARKLE ♥!

HEADBANDS

MADE OF CLOTH LOOK EXTRA ADORABLE PINNED WITH FLOWERS OR AN ANTIQUE PIN, ♥ & YOU CAN DO THE SAME THING WITH A SCARF IN YOUR HAIR.

There is another reason for dressing well, namely that dogs respect it & will not attack you in good clothes. ♥ *Ralph Waldo Emerson*

A WAIST IS A TERRIBLE THING TO MIND, SO IF YOU DON'T REALLY HAVE ONE, LOOK FOR DRESSES WITH LOWER OR HIGHER (EMPIRE) WAISTLINES. SHOULDER PADS ALSO MAKE YOU LOOK LIKE YOU HAVE A WAIST. ALL ONE COLOR, SHOES, TIGHTS, SKIRT, JACKET, WILL THIN AND L E N G T H E N YOU— THEN TIE ON A GREAT SCARF OR NECKLACE TO BRING ATTENTION TO YOUR GORGEOUS FACE, BEAUTIFUL SMILE, AND TWINKLING EYES. ♥

There is entirely too much charm around & something must be done to stop it. ♥ Dorothy Parker

I LEARNED THIS FROM 1950'S TEEN-AGE MOVIES — THAT A BEAUTIFUL FINE-GAUGE CARDIGAN SWEATER CAN BE VERY CUTE TURNED AROUND & BUTTONED UP THE BACK. ♥

Little Snax: BIGGER SLAX.

NOTICE TO WOMEN'S CLOTHING STORES OF AMERICA:

SEW SPARKLY BUGLE BEADS ON FOR DRESS-UP

IF YOU WOULD PLEASE REMOVE FLUORESCENT LIGHTING FROM THE DRESSING ROOMS, YOU WOULD SELL ALOT MORE BATHING SUITS. SPEAKING FOR THE WOMEN OF AMERICA—

I thank you ♥

CLEAN YOUR HAIRBRUSH OUTSIDE SO BIRDS CAN MAKE NESTS FROM YOUR TOUSLES. ♥

FLAT FRONT PANTS CONTROL A POOCHY STOMACH BETTER THAN PLEATED PANTS (WHICH JUST SEEM TO ALLOW FOR THE PLACE TO PUT THE POOCH! ♥).

Styles, like everything else, change. Style doesn't.
♥ LINDA ELLERBEE

When shopping, ask yourself, "is this fad or classic?" Classic is timeless & you'll wear it FOREVER, so that's where the money should go: sunglasses, jeans, jacket, purse, shoes, & HAIRCUT — the things you wear every day are the most important. But fads are fun & FUN is GOOD. ♥

Women are most fascinating
between the ages of 35 and 40 after they
have won a few races & know how to
pace themselves. Since few women ever
pass 40, maximum fascination can continue
indefinitely. ♥ Christian Dior

SELF-RESPECT

Never give up. ♥ Style is discipline & constancy; it's not about money or beauty. At the market the other day, I noticed a tiny woman who seemed to glow.

She was dressed simply but what I loved was the ribbon she'd tied in her hair ~ joie de vivre in action. ♥ Taking a guess, I'd say she was about 80 years young. She's my inspiration ~ I want to be just like her when I grow up.

Years are only garments & you either wear them with STYLE all your life, or you go dowdy to the grave.
— Dorothy Parker

My mother was always so proud of us ~ she liked for us to get dressed up for holidays & for church. Our family pictures show her good influence ~ in one I wear white gloves that have a ruffle. ♥ It was part of her understanding of self-respect ~ a sweet desire to do her part, and make this world a better place by having clean children. The only fashion advice I really remember her giving was: "ALWAYS WEAR CLEAN UNDERWEAR IN CASE YOU'RE IN AN ACCIDENT."

What is self-respect? You could write a book! But basically it's the care of character & conduct. Treating yourself like you MATTER, with esteem. Eating healthy food, exercising, getting regular medical check ups, developing spirituality, learning about money, using manners, keeping a clean house ~ self-respect makes you beautiful at any age. ♥

Pride is a necessary quality for a person ~ not vain or pompous pride, but basic honest pride in self, family, home, work & country. With it you will always stand tall. ♥ James A. Retzlaff

BE GOOD TO YOURSELF

SHUNNING THE UPSTART SHOWER,
THE COLD & CURSORY SCRUB,
I CELEBRATE THE POWER
THAT LIES WITHIN THE TUB.
♥ *Phyllis McGinley*

LOLL ABOUT · SOOTHE · PAMPER · SPOIL · UNWIND · AND COMFORT YOURSELF · MEDITATE · ADD HOT WATER · STAY AWHILE · LOCK THE DOOR · JUST THE SIMPLE THINGS IN LIFE ·

What you need: bubble bath, or bath salts,
a big bottle of cold water to drink, music
(or none), & a good book (or not). ♥

READ A FUNNY BOOK ~ LAUGHTER IS SUCH GOOD MEDICINE!
TRY DAVE BARRY TALKS BACK ~ hilarious!

I can't think of any sorrow in the world
that a hot bath wouldn't help, just a
little bit. ♥ *Susan Glaspell*

48

EGG WHITE Facial

In a small bowl, whip the white of one egg lightly with a fork till frothy. Spread over face (not too close to skin around eyes). Lie down & think good thoughts till it dries completely. Rinse well in tepid water.

A BATH IS FOR RELAXING BUT A SHOWER LEAVES YOU ENERGIZED & SPARKLING CLEAN. A LOOFAH OR PUFF PUFF IS A BIG HELP BECAUSE THEY REMOVE OLD DRY SKIN BUT A THICK TERRY WASHCLOTH WORKS JUST AS WELL. EITHER WAY, WITH A GOOD PURE PLAIN SOAP LIKE IVORY WORK UP A THICK SOAPY LATHER IN THE WASHCLOTH AND SCRUB EVERY CREVICE, BACK OF KNEES, BEHIND EARS, BETWEEN TOES AND THEN RINSE AND RINSE AND RINSE (COOL WATER TIGHTENS PORES MAKES YOU GLOW) THEN A GOOD SMELLING BODY CREAM FOR FROSTING ON YOU.

SOME PEOPLE LIKE A STOOL IN THE SHOWER

SHAMPOO

49

Build a ladder to the stars & climb up every rung & may you stay forever young. ♥ Joan Baez

Natural Beauty

With your face still warm from your bath, apply this moisturizing mask: in a blender put 1 c. mashed strawberries, 2 tbsp. cream, 2 tbsp. cornstarch ~ blend till smooth (ish). Spread on face, leave on 20 min., rinse with warm water.

Calm your frizzies & moisturize your hair: heat 1/4 c. olive oil till it's just warm ~ oil can burn so be very careful. Massage into dry hair, wrap head in a damp, warm towel & wait 15 min. Shampoo. (You'll have to shampoo a couple of times to get it all out but it really does the job.)

Save used tea bags, chill them, place one on each eye ~ lay down for 15 min. Reduces puffiness & clears redness.

Keep an eye on your birthday suit ~ make sure freckles aren't going haywire, visit a Dermatologist regularly. Get tan with sunless tanning cream.

To heal rough hands & feet, soak them in warm water; rub Vaseline all over, put on cotton socks or gloves & take your little self to bed.

To whiten fingernails plunge them into a lemon half.

"I TRIED AROMATHERAPY. IT STUNK." ♥ Anon. (THE BEST AROMATHERAPY I KNOW OF IS SOMETHING COOKING ON THE STOVE, OR CHOCOLATE CHIP COOKIES BAKING IN THE OVEN ~ NOW THAT'S WHAT I CALL THERAPY ♥)

HOW TO BE PULLED TOGETHER WHEN TRAVELING

It takes a little planning but it's worth it if you need to look good when you get where you're going. ♥

Try on your clothes before you go ~ put together some cute outfits & write everything down, including accessories ~ then make sure it all gets packed! This way you'll have the striped socks that go best with the wide-leg pants & the woven bag will be there too. Be sure to include your "outfit list" in the suitcase so you'll know what you've got when you get there. ♥ Like this:

WHITE LINEN JUMPER
WHITE T-SHIRT
PINK FRUIT SHOES
SHELL EARRINGS
PINK/WH. PEARL BRACELET
ROSE PIN
PINK PEARL RING

FISH T-SHIRT
GREEN FLOWERED SKIRT
LAURA ASHLEY SLIP
GREEN LIZARD SANDALS
LINEN JACKET
IVORY/PINK BRACELET
CAMEO RINGS

MATERIAL GIRLS

IF YOUR OUTGO EXCEEDS YOUR INCOME,
YOUR UPKEEP WILL BE YOUR DOWNFALL.
♥ Anon.

An alternative to Quilting Bees are Investment Clubs ~ where people get together to learn about finance and investing. As more women gain control of their own money (& therefore their own destinies), they are realizing that besides ensuring personal independence, money is a primary weapon for fighting injustice.

Money, like power, can be a devil or an angel & it all depends on who holds the purse strings & what they value. You are never too young or too old to learn about money.

Socially Responsible Investing

There are pro-fitable mutual funds that invest only in companies that are good for the earth & for people. The stocks in these funds are thoroughly researched so investors can be assured they are not supporting nuclear proliferation, polluters, tobacco, companies with poor records on equal opportunity, or companies that rely on child labor.

With our dollars we can support good things; protect the earth, defend women & children, & change the world. ♡

I don't know much about being a millionaire, but I bet I'd be darling at it.
♥ Dorothy Parker

FOR MORE INFORMATION
www.domini.com
www.socialfunds.com

I HAVE ENOUGH MONEY TO LAST ME THE REST OF MY LIFE, AS LONG AS I DON'T BUY ANYTHING. ♥ Anon.

WEB SITES for WOMEN

www.esteemedwoman.com
smartparent.com
switchboard.com
epicurious.com
garden.com
realastrology.com
familysearch.com
ms.foundation.org
womenswire.com
citizensfunds.com
consumerreports.com
ebay.com
mayohealth.org
and susanbranch.com

P.S. Supporting women in politics (whose ideas you agree with of course) is also a way to make a change because, as Jeannette Rankin said, "We're half the people, we should be half the Congress."

...Where even the
teakettle sings from
happiness.
That is Home.
♥ Ernestine Schumann-Heink

THE ART of the HOME

When I was 10 or 11 one of the games I used to want to play with the neighborhood girls was "Let's go home & decorate our bedrooms." (To be honest, I was the ONLY one who liked this game!) I tried to make my room look like the "teenager" rooms I saw in _Seventeen_ Magazine, so I would fan out record albums onto my white cotton shag throw rugs just like they did (even tho' I didn't have a record player in my room :·). My dad made me a dressing table out of 2 orange crates & a board he covered in faux marble drawer paper & my mother made a skirt for it, gathered in yellow dotted Swiss that (to me) was as beautiful as a prom dress ♥. I learned I could have anything I wanted as long as I could make it. I copied things & got ideas from magazines until I gained confidence & learned to be creative on my own. ♥

"And each heart is whispering
'Home, Home at last!'"
♥ Thomas Hood

Homemaking is the most creative job there is — we're always making something from nothing! It's cooking, decorating, gardening, arranging & planning — not to mention child care, which requires a Michelangelo of Creativity — all true arts ♥. It's hard for most of us to have as much time for it as we once did, but we do still love our homes — love a cozy, nurturing environment, love seeing ourselves reflected in our things. Making a home for ourselves & our families is second nature to most of us — it's the place where love grows ♥. →

THE ART OF THE HOME, CON'T.

In the spirit of full disclosure I should tell you I am definitely not a minimalist. I do like looking at pictures of that clean serene way of decorating, but my question is always "What about my STUFF?" Real life is not going to allow me to put everything away just to be fashionable. Not set out my teapots? I don't THINK so! I need my stuff so I have something to paint in my books!

Here's a few ideas ~ I'm sure you have plenty of good ones yourself ~ the beauty of it is that "home" is personal expression. ♥ There's no wrong way.

IDEAS: Ask your grandma for old family photos to frame; hang quilts (gorgeous colors!) on chairs, over backs of couches, draped over the foot of the bed, hung on quilt racks. Hang pretty China plates on the wall, display cups & bowls in old hutches, put teapots on the mantle. I collect dishes so when I moved into my house my Dad (Mr. Handy ♥) took the doors totally off my kitchen cupboards. Use old tablecloths, hang dishtowels on oven doors. Pretty lamps, soft lighting, lots of candles with sparkling glass or wooden candle holders; flowered wallpaper, clocks that tick, wonderful music & a fire in the fireplace. Couch pillows in pretty fabrics, fresh flowered sheets & fluffy comforters. Lots of books & photo albums; a collection of old mismatched wine glasses. Ah yes... collections: dolls, teacups, door stops, wooden spoons, old Beatrix Potter figurines, straw hats,

salt & pepper shakers, you could go on forever! Collections from nature for your window sills: seashells, beach glass, rocks, starfish, & pinecones. Mirrors make rooms lighter & bigger. Homemade things & children's art— I love the pottery handprints hanging from satin ribbons in my mother's kitchen. Add trim to plain things: rick-rack, embroidery & ribbon to dishtowels, bath towels or pillow cases. Baskets; bowls of fresh fruit — lemons, peaches, pears, apples add color. Try a row of yellow apples on a window sill. And FLOWERS — everywhere! In charming pots & vases you collected yourself. Old-fashioned curtains & little hooked rugs & needlepointed things. And don't forget the outside! Door decorations & wreaths, pots of flowers on the porch, trellises full of roses, a straw hat hung on your garden gate, bird feeders, bird baths & bird houses. Flowering trees: crabapple, dogwood, magnolia; & bushes: lilac & hydrangea. ♥ A place to have dinner under the stars. And if you live alone you should consider a cat or a dog or a bird — they are love & it's love that makes a house a home. Remember it's not about perfection — if you do it with heart — that's art. ♥ The art of the home. ♥

Redecorating can be done on zero money & it can PAY! Here's how: empty a whole room of everything but the furniture; remove curtains, pictures, everything. Clean the room then start with your favorite things & put back just one plumped, cleaned & sparkled piece at a time. When it looks perfect, STOP. Put everything else you love away (for redecorating another time) & have a yard sale for the rest. (My best friend & I did this; cleaned our houses, had a joint yard sale & bought ourselves 2 tickets to Hawaii with the money we made — Aloha-ha! ☺) ♥

57

TWO HAPPY WAHINES ON VACATION →

REAL LIFE
Good Housekeeping

IF YOUR HOUSE IS REALLY A MESS & A STRANGER COMES TO THE DOOR, GREET HER WITH, "WHO COULD HAVE DONE THIS? WE HAVE NO ENEMIES." ♥ PHYLLIS DILLER

QUICK CLEAN

SURPRISE GUESTS? YOU'LL BE AMAZED AT WHAT YOU CAN DO IN 10 MINUTES. ♥

• Hide all clutter ~ run around, pick it all up, & throw it all into a closet.

• Get the dirty dishes out of sight ~ load the dishwasher, wipe kitchen table & counters.

• Feather-dust rooms that show.
Vacuum open spaces (if there's time) neatly shake little rugs & lay them over the dirt; "dustbust" crumbs, cat food on kitchen floor.

• Close the shower curtain! Wipe down mirrors, sink, & chrome w/ a hot wash cloth. Straighten towels (turn them around), flush the toilet & close the lid.

• Only do the rooms you'll be using & close the doors to the rest.

• Extra time? Do detail work, especially in the kitchen where everybody always ends up.

NEED INSPIRATION TO CLEAN UP YOUR HOUSE? GIVE A PARTY!

I buried a lot of my ironing in the backyard.
♥ Phyllis Diller

Sweep your house (or room) counter-clockwise & you'll sweep out any negative energy.

THE BEST NEW ROOM IN THE HOUSE
Creativity is really the structuring of magic.
♥ ANNE KENT RUSH

So make a "magic room" ~ a craft room. Have wide surfaces to work on, a place to keep wrapping paper & ribbon ~ organize things so you can get to them, according to your interests ~ stickers, scrapbooks, glue, glitter, colored pencils, pinking shears, hole punch, construction paper, rubber stamps, journals, stationery, fabric, yarn, ribbons, buttons, watercolors, how-to books, the sewing machine & files for collecting ideas. Decorate with your own collections ~ have music & a good chair for dreaming in. ♥

The imagination needs moodling, ~ long, inefficient, happy idling, dawdling and puttering.
♥ Brenda Ueland

"Nothing feeds the center of being so much as creative work. The curtain of mechanization has come down between the mind & the hand."
♡ Anne Morrow Lindbergh

Creativity

I read the other day that the "keys to a successful future for our daughters include a comfort with math & science, the mastering of technology, an understanding of money & finance, with an emphasis on career goals." A great list, but I don't want us to forget creative expression. Life wouldn't be much fun if it was all one big push-a-button computerized moment. Girls (& boys!) are naturally creative little beings, but creativity needs nurturing too. The things you love in your childhood you love all your life. Most craft stores offer special classes for children (& adults). Hobbies raise levels of self-confidence, bring pleasure, provide solace, & are a great way for people to feel they have something of themselves to Give. There are so many soul-satisfying ways of self-expression — here are just a few:

DEAR DIARY

"Christmas Eve 1977 11:40 am — raining. It's rained the last 3 days straight — I have cookies baking in the oven & I'm still in my jammies. We're having a party to-night. Kitty just caught & devoured her Christmas fly..."

... and with that entry I began what (so far) is the 17 books of my life. My diaries don't only include

turn the page

P.s. Addendum to last entry. Joe & I walked out to fleeing Creek. This am ran into Melissa & Bob (2 doors from our beach house) who stood on their porch & recited (serenaded!) us together with this poem they had written:

"Gathered amidst the arbored grounds
Cast a setting for new friends found
Hand held sparklers lit up the night
Distant fireworks, an added delight
Dinner served with elegant ease
Delicious food certain to please.
Umbrellas held high to shield the rain
With voices joined in sweet refrain
Thank you for sharing your humulus
We certainly appreciate all the fuss."
I forgot to mention that we all joined in singing The Star Spangled Banner, spontaneously, but with gusto!

C E L E B R A T E ♡
The 1st dinner party of 1999... Saturday, January 2, 1999
We had 12 - Joe, Sue, Shelly, Thomas Cox, Dana, Susie Frees, Victor & Judy, Tosh & Jeannie McIntosh, Michael Rouff + Larry Lenska ...just put those names in a beautiful candle lit dining room & you have got yourself wit, charm & beauty &
FUN
FUN
FUN

T I M E F L Y S →

con't.

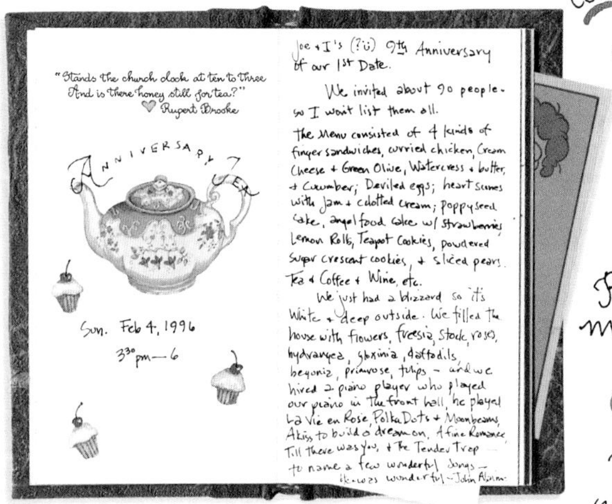

my musings but are decorated with quotes, photographs, good horoscopes, newspaper articles, stickers, restaurant napkins, historical notes, ticket stubs, dried flowers & drawings. Babies are born, pets go to heaven, heartbreak heals, little moments matter, & growing up occurs.

Anybody can keep a journal & you don't need to be Steinbeck to do it. It doesn't matter what you write or how you write as long as you tell the truth because this book is for you♥.

There are also small journals for special occasions. Pictured is the little book I keep to record dinner parties in. You could also do special vacations, a new house book, men I have known & loved, favorite outfits for special occassions, 1st year of marriage including honeymoon, or a family trip. As many of you know, the older your journals & scrapbooks get, the more valuable they become. ♥

It's not that I belong to the past, but that the past belongs to me. ♥ Mary Antin

Create a Garden

We cut our kitchen garden right out of the center of our lawn & put a picket fence all the way around it. ♥ Here are some ideas for other gardens ♥

Butterfly Garden
The Secret Garden
Potted Garden
Perennial Garden
Cutting Garden
White Garden
Wildflower Garden
Hummingbird Garden
Water Garden
Meditation Garden
Herb Garden
Rose Garden
Knot Garden

TO PLANT A SEED IS A HOPEFUL DEED

Rock Garden

YOU THINK OF SOME ♥

The inset journal page reads:

"Stands the church clock at ten to three
And is there honey still for tea?"
♥ Rupert Brooke

ANNIVERSARY TEA

Sun. Feb 4, 1996
3:30 pm — 6

Joe & I's (?'s) 9th Anniversary & our 1st Date.

We invited about 90 people — so I won't list them all.

The menu consisted of 4 kinds of finger sandwiches, curried chicken, Cream Cheese & Green Olive, Watercress & butter, & Cucumber, Deviled eggs; heart scones with Jam & clotted cream; Poppyseed Cake, angel food cake w/ strawberries, Lemon Rolls, Teapot Cookies, powdered Sugar crescent cookies, & sliced pears! Tea & Coffee & Wine, etc.

We just had a blizzard so it's white & deep outside. We filled the house with flowers, freesia, stock, roses, hydrangea, gardenia, daffodils, begonia, primrose, tulips — and we hired a piano player who played our piano in the front hall. He played La Vie en Rose, Polka Dots & Moonbeams, Ain't to build a dream on, A fine Romance, Till there was you, & the Tender Trap to name a few wonderful songs. It was wonderful. ~ John Alden

LITTLE IDEAS

Recipe Boxes often end up as treasured family heirlooms. Include recipes from family members & they become historical! Tuck in kitchen hints, quotes; cut out pictures to glue onto cards ~ even photos, & kids' chocolate fingerprints ~ memories are made of this ♥.

Seed Packets Collect seeds from wisteria, foxglove, poppies, etc. (or get them at the store!) & package them in tiny gift-card envelopes. Decorated with stickers or stamps, they make a charming gift tucked into a card or a book.

MARTHA'S VINEYARD POPPIES

A CHARM BRACELET celebrates life & tells stories ~ besides regular charms, I also use small mementos ~ my baby bracelet, a charm my Dad gave to my mom, a cuff link from the QE I that Joe gave me ~ & the bracelet itself is a watch fob that also used to belong to Joe. ♥

FENCE ME IN

Garden Party Dessert: Makes the table look darling. Get some new small clay pots ~ boil them for 15 min. (start them in cold water). Fill them with ice cream, crumble chocolate cookies over to look like dirt. Insert a straw deep into ice cream & cut off just at "dirt" level. Keep in freezer. Just before serving insert a long-stemmed flower into straw. Pass w/ chocolate or berry sauce. ♥

Outdoor Lighting for dinner parties is a great place to be creative ~ there are so many ways to go: tiki torches, colorful Chinese lanterns, luminarias, colored glass ~ & this lamp, the wind can't blow out. Get a big glass container & put sand in the bottom. Sink a fat candle in the sand & surround it w/ seashells, beach glass or starfish. Bring it inside for the holidays & do berries, pinecones ~ little ornaments.

A toast to us my good fat friends,
To bless the things we eat;
For it has been full many a year,
Since we have seen our feet:
Yet who would lose a precious pound,
By trading sweets for sours?
It takes a mighty girth indeed,
To hold such hearts as ours!

— Wallace Irwin

CRUNCHY, SALADY, VIBRANT, Wholesome & DEE-LICIOUS ♥
(OTHER PEOPLE HAVE BEEN KNOWN TO ENJOY THIS KIND OF FOOD
TOO, BUT I CALL IT :)

GIRL FOOD

Lead me
not
into temptation;
I can find the way
myself.
♥ Rita Mae Brown

P O W E R

"WE'VE SEEN THE FUTURE, AND THE FUTURE IS FOOD." ♥ DR. MITCHELL GAYNOR, HEAD OF MEDICAL ONCOLOGY AT NEW YORK'S STRANG CANCER PREVENTION CENTER

Ongoing research brings more good news about food every day ~ that it's BALANCE & VARIETY that's best for us ~ & that eating a diet rich in these POWER FOODS may actually help boost our immune systems & prevent disease.

THE NUTRITIONAL SUPERSTARS
EAT FOR HEALTH

TOMATOES: *cooking* TOMATOES RELEASES GOOD LYCOPENE ~ ADDING OLIVE OIL TO IT HELPS CARRY IT INTO THE BLOODSTREAM.

BROCCOLI CAULIFLOWER CABBAGE SWEET POTATOES SPINACH BRUSSELS SPROUTS

GARLIC CHIVES & ONIONS

SPROUTS: ALFALFA, BEAN & BROCCOLI

GOOD OILS:
CANOLA
FLAXSEED
OLIVE
WALNUT

TOFU
SOY MILK
TEMPEH

RED GRAPES
CANTALOUPE
CITRUS FRUITS
ALL BERRIES
WATERMELON

FISH IS BRAIN FOOD
SALMON, TUNA, TROUT, BLUEFISH, SARDINES, MACKEREL
TAKE SOME OF YOUR CANDY MONEY, DIAL 1-800-394-6071 & BUY THE FRESHEST FISH POSSIBLE - MAIL ORDER FROM MARTHA'S VINEYARD. ♥

GREEN TEA ICED OR HOT (TRY LIPTON'S OR CELESTIAL SEASONINGS W/ ORANGE, PASSION FRUIT, & JASMINE MMMMM)

SLOW-COOKED OATMEAL

F O O D S

DARK LEAFY GREENS, CARROTS (BEST COOKED),
COLORFUL PEPPERS

GROUND FLAXSEED &
WHEATGERM:
SPRINKLE ON CEREAL,
BLEND INTO TURKEY
BURGERS, MEATLOAF

BEANS

PAPAYA
MANGOES
KIWI FRUIT
TANGERINES

NUTS

DRINK LOTS of WATER

ABOUT TOFU

For a long time the reason for tofu escaped me ~ it was a complete mystery ~ what *was* it anyway? It didn't even *look* like food. But the well-touted benefits made me curious. So here's what I found out: Tofu is soybeans; soaked, pureed, & cooked down to soy milk, then pressed into cake form. It is so high in protein that it can easily substitute for meat or dairy ~ but it is low calorie, low fat, & has no cholesterol. It helps fight heart disease & cancer & seems to balance hormones, especially estrogen. It has almost no flavor by itself~ but picks up the flavors of whatever you serve it with in a very nice way. Chunk the "firm" kind into spaghetti sauce, soups, casseroles, salads, & stir-fries ~ slice it into sandwiches. Children & husbands won't even know it's there! ♥

65

FOOD FROM THE HEART
AND FOR IT, TOO!

Every day they find out about food-as-almost-medicine & these are the "Power Foods" I concentrated on for this book ~ great-tasting recipes that deliver a nutritional punch ~ crunchy vegetables, satisfying proteins, juicy fruits, & comforting starches that are VIBRANT & ALIVE & make us feel that way. Lower in fat, higher in satisfaction but it's the nurturing love in food that makes it so important & that's what you provide.

An Interesting Conundrum

If it's OK to spend $4.00 on a quart of "Chubby Hubby," $7.00 on Sarah Lee & $3.00 on a six-pack of Coke, Why isn't it OK to spend a little extra to fill your fridge with the best of everything that's good for you? Instead of ice cream, cakes, potato chips, pies, pop, donuts & butter ~ fill your fridge with organic veggies, berries (out of season!), fresh lobster & shrimp, best olive oils, Farmers Market asparagus & blueberries; sushi & other pre-made delights from the "healthy" market; freshly squeezed juices & flowers for your table. (Because YOU, MY DEAREST ONES, ARE WORTH IT!)

"Self respect is a question of recognizing that anything worth having has its price."

♥ Joan Didion

66

HOW TO EAT HEALTHY
WHEN THERE IS NO TIME

Eating well does require extra time no matter what anybody says — time to shop, chop, wash & plan. To make it SO MUCH EASIER, choose one day a week (like Sunday afternoon) & do "supplement" cooking: make a pot of soup, roast a chicken, steam some shrimp, cut up veggies, wash lettuce, or make a main dish salad. Put some cottage cheese, apples & red grapes in the fridge for quick snacks. The temptation for easy grabs like chips will be lessened & you'll have a week's worth of fabulous "fast food" at your fingertips. ♥

Oh, nooo, NOT THAT AGAIN!

I keep a kind of "menu" in my purse. It looks like this. So when I'm at the market & I want something special, I just pull out my list & all the ingred. are right there! (I don't bother to list staples, things I always have on hand, just the fresh stuff.) I usually have 10-12 recipes on my "menu" & I change it seasonally. It's especially great in the summer — for SPONTANEOUS entertaining — no muss, no fuss — & it keeps us from eating the same things every night. ♥

FISH TACOS
⅓ lb. cod (for 2)
tortillas
red onion
limes
avocado
tomato
cilantro

MANGO SALAD
2 limes
3 mangos
red pepper
red onion
mint
cilantro

MASHED POTATOES
potatoes
buttermilk
garlic

MEATLOAF
1 c onion
celery
carrots
mushrooms
eggs
gr. onion
parsley
br. crumbs
1¼ lb. turkey

CHEESE BITES
parmesan
red onion

BEAN SALAD
½ lb. wh. beans
celery
red onion
parsley
anchovies

67

"I have been on a constant
diet for the last 2 decades.
I've lost a total of 789 pounds. By all
accounts I should be hanging from a
charm bracelet."

Erma Bombeck

NO FAT! EAT BREAD! . . .  TIME PASSES . . . NO BREAD! EAT FAT!

TODAY IF YOU'RE NOT CONFUSED YOU'RE JUST NOT THINKING CLEARLY. ♥ Irene Peter

"CERTAINLY." HE BEAMED UNCERTAINLY. "CERTAINLY." ♥ Holly Roth

Here are 2 yummy crisped breads to serve with soups, salads, dips, salsas, & as croutons ♥.

SEEDED PITA CRISPS

71 CAL. · 2 G. FAT · 12 G. CARBO.   Serves 6 (MAKES 32 PIECES)

2 pita breads   2 tsp. poppy seeds
olive oil spray   1 tsp. Parmesan cheese
2 tsp. sesame seeds   a sprinkle of paprika
        salt & freshly ground pepper

Preheat oven to 350°. Cut pitas into 8 wedges, then separate each wedge into 2 pieces. Arrange on baking sheet & spray lightly w/ olive oil; sprinkle all other ingred. evenly over tops. Bake for 10 min. ♥

TIP: INSTEAD OF BUTTER, DIP CRUSTY BREAD IN A LITTLE PUDDLE OF OLIVE OIL SEASONED W/ S & P & SOME FRESH ROSEMARY LEAVES ♥.

GARLICKY BAGEL TOASTS

65 CAL. · LESS THAN 1 GR. FAT · 13 G. CARBO · Serves 6 (MAKES 14 PIECES)

2 lg. bagels   1 lg. clove garlic
        spray olive oil

Preheat oven to 350°. Cut bagels into ¼" slices. (CAREFULLY!) Rub pieces with a halved garlic clove & arrange on baking sheet. Spray lightly with olive oil. Bake 15 min.

TAKE NOTE:

Bread that must be sliced with an ax is bread that is too nourishing. ♥

hi-yahh!   FRAN LEBOWITZ

69

YAYA MUNCHIES

I NO LONGER PREPARE FOOD OR
DRINK WITH MORE THAN ONE INGREDIENT.
♥ CYRA M°FADDEN

HARD-BOILED EGGS

DRIED APRICOTS

CANTALOUPE PIECES

A SMALL CAN OF TUNA FISH

and A CARROT

AN ARTICHOKE WITH
LEMON JUICE

Celery Sticks

HOT TEA AT 4 O'CLOCK

A THINLY SLICED APPLE
FOR ALL-DAY MUNCHING

A LITTLE PILE OF
CHOCOLATE BITS

ICED RADISHES

SALSA WITH AK-MAK CRACKERS

FIG COOKIE

STEAMED SHRIMP W/ LEMON

RED GRAPES

IF YOU'RE OUT & ABOUT

HAVE A CAFFE LATTE MADE
WITH 1% MILK, OH! SO! GOOD!

V-8 W/ LEMON

A PIECE OF CHICKEN

♥ ½ C. CANNED ORGANIC

APPLESAUCE & ½ C.

LOW-FAT COTTAGE CHEESE:

(A LITTLE BIT OF BOTH

ON THE FORK— YUM)

FINGERS WERE MADE BEFORE FORKS
♥ Jonathan Swift

VELVET CHICKEN
With SPICY LIME DIP

1 GR. FAT PER 5 DIPPED PIECES · 131 CALORIES · 195 MG. SODIUM · 15 G. PROTEIN · 16 G. CARBO

Makes 60 pieces

TGIF for my girlfriends is a talking good-fest — we solve all the world's problems every Friday night ☺. ♡

They Loved This ↙

2 lbs. skinless, boneless chicken breasts, cut into bite-sized pieces

½ tsp. salt
1 Tbsp. light soy sauce
4 Tbsp. cornstarch
2 egg whites

> THERE IS NOTHING WRONG WITH THE WORLD THAT A SENSIBLE WOMAN COULD NOT SETTLE IN AN AFTERNOON. ♥
> — JEAN GIRAUDOUX

Bring 3 qt. water to boil, add salt & soy sauce. In a med. bowl whisk together cornstarch & egg whites & stir in chicken pieces. Fill a large bowl with ice & water & set aside. Set a colander in the sink. Add chicken to boiling water & stir to separate. As soon as it comes back to full boil remove from heat & let stand 1 min. Quickly check a piece for doneness. Drain in colander & immediately plunge chicken into ice water. Let sit for 2 min. Drain. Arrange on a platter with a bowl of dip; garnish with lime slices & cilantro leaves. ♥

Dip: 8 oz. lime marmalade; heaping ¼ c. horseradish; 3 Tbsp. chopped cilantro; 2 Tbsp. minced fresh ginger. Melt marmalade in a small saucepan over med. heat. Remove from heat; stir in all ingredients. Chill. ♥ Use toothpicks for dipping.

71

This has been a most wonderful evening. Gertrude has said things tonight it will take her ten years to understand. ♥ *Alice B. Toklas*

GRILLED CALAMARI

116 CAL • 2 G. FAT • 18 G. PROTEIN   8 G. CARBO. • 50 MG. SODIUM • 0 G. FIBER

Serves 8

Much better than deep-fried! Also great on a green salad ~ pure protein ♥.

2 lbs. calamari, cleaned
olive oil spray

salt & freshly ground pepper
2 limes, cut into wedges

Pat calamari dry, leave whole. Lightly spray dish with olive oil, sprinkle w/ s. & p., sauté quickly (3-4 min.) in a very hot, olive-oil-sprayed, ridged grill pan (see p. 100). Careful not to over cook, turn once or twice. Remove from heat, cut into rings & serve w/ lime wedges. ♥

ROASTED GARLIC

Squeeze onto salads, into vegetables, into soups & dips, spread onto crackers ~ have it w/ goat cheese & red wine ♥.

FLAVOR & HEALTH BENEFITS GALORE

½-1 head garlic per person, olive oil, & fresh rosemary &/or thyme. Preheat oven to 350°. Cut off top ⅓ of garlic head, exposing all cloves. Put them (heads) in a small baking dish. Drizzle over ¼ tsp. olive oil per head. Sprinkle over minced herbs. Cover dish w/ aluminum foil & bake 1 hr. ♥

At TGIF lately, we've been talking about genetically altered food ~ we're against it! If you are too, call 202/224-3121; ask for the ph. # of your Senator or Congressperson (they even know WHO he is) & EXPRESS YOURSELF. ♥

♪ WE ARE THE WORLD, WE ARE THE CHILDREN... ♪

FINGER-LICKIN' GOOD!

Dry Bones

PER 1 LG. or 3 SM: 66 CAL. · 6 G. FAT · 4 G. PROTEIN
ZERO CARBOS   375° Makes 6 lbs.

These ribs are dry, crunchy & delicious & they give everyone something to chew on. This recipe works for either the large rack or the smaller appetizer ribs. ♥

2 tsp. ground sage
1 tsp. dried thyme
1/4 tsp. cayenne pepper
2 tsp. salt
2 tsp. freshly ground pepper
6 lbs. pork ribs

Preheat oven to 375°. Blend together first 5 ingred. Rub mixture over both sides of racks of ribs & put them on a baking sheet. Roast 1/2 hr., turn, then continue cooking another 45 min. to 1 hr. till brown & done ♥.

IT IS THE DUTY OF YOUTH TO BRING ITS FRESH NEW POWERS TO BEAR ON SOCIAL PROGRESS. EACH GENERATION OF YOUNG PEOPLE SHOULD BE TO THE WORLD LIKE A VAST RESERVE FORCE TO A TIRED ARMY. THEY SHOULD LIFT THE WORLD FORWARD. THAT IS WHAT THEY ARE FOR.

♥ Charlotte Perkins Gilman

HOLY MOLE

62 CAL · LESS THAN 1 G. FAT · 4 G. PROTEIN · 69 MG. SODIUM · 12 G. CARBO · 3 G. FIBER

Serves 8 (3 cups)

This looks, smells, & tastes *exactly* like Guacamole (which has about 60 G. of fat in a normal bowlful) but it's *not*, it's peas! (Holy Mole! or Guacapeamole!) Easy! Serve with Ak Mak crackers or Seeded Pita Crisps (p. 69). ♥

1 lb. bag frozen baby peas
½ c. red onion, minced
¼ c. cilantro, finely chopped
2 green onions, minced
2 cloves garlic, pressed
1 jalapeño, minced, or ¼ tsp. cayenne
½ tsp. cumin
1 Tbsp. red wine vinegar
1 lg. tomato, diced
zest of 1 lime
salt & freshly ground pepper, to taste

Drop frozen peas in boiling water ~ cook 1 min., drain. Rinse w/cold water & let dry. Puree peas well in processor. Remove to bowl & stir in remaining ingredients. Chill. ♥

ONE OUT OF EVERY FOUR PEOPLE IN THIS COUNTRY IS MENTALLY IMBALANCED. THINK OF YOUR THREE CLOSEST FRIENDS ~ AND IF THEY SEEM OKAY, THEN YOU'RE THE ONE. ♥ Ann Landers

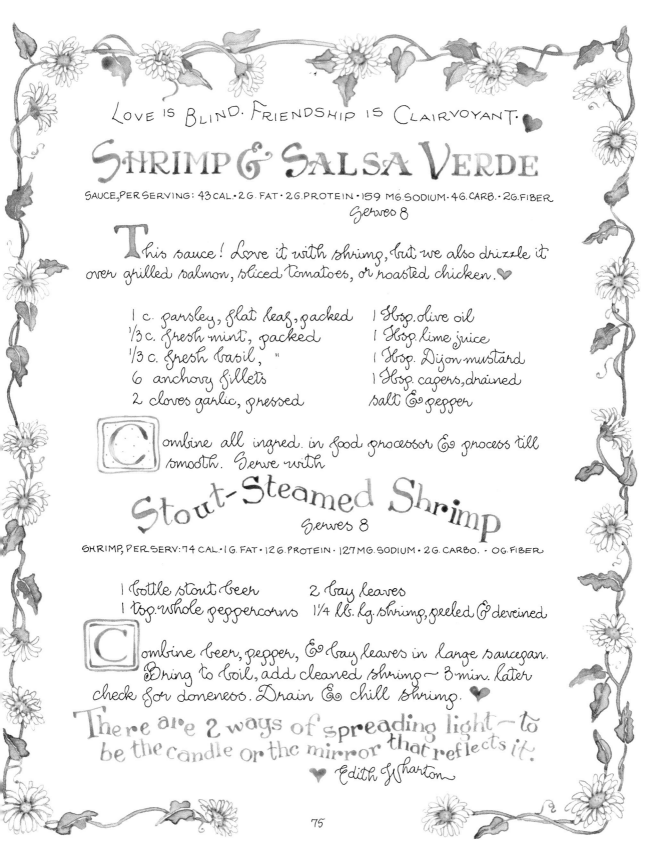

LOVE IS BLIND. FRIENDSHIP IS CLAIRVOYANT. ♥

SHRIMP & SALSA VERDE

SAUCE, PER SERVING: 43 CAL. · 2 G. FAT · 2 G. PROTEIN · 159 MG. SODIUM · 4 G. CARB. · 2 G. FIBER

Serves 8

This sauce! Love it with shrimp, but we also drizzle it over grilled salmon, sliced tomatoes, or roasted chicken. ♥

1 c. parsley, flat leaf, packed	1 Tbsp. olive oil
1/3 c. fresh mint, packed	1 Tbsp. lime juice
1/3 c. fresh basil, "	1 Tbsp. Dijon mustard
6 anchovy fillets	1 Tbsp. capers, drained
2 cloves garlic, pressed	salt & pepper

Combine all ingred. in food processor & process till smooth. Serve with

Stout-Steamed Shrimp

Serves 8

SHRIMP, PER SERV: 74 CAL. · 1 G. FAT · 12 G. PROTEIN · 127 MG. SODIUM · 2 G. CARBO. · 0 G. FIBER

1 bottle stout beer	2 bay leaves
1 tsp. whole peppercorns	1¼ lb. lg. shrimp, peeled & deveined

Combine beer, pepper, & bay leaves in large saucepan. Bring to boil, add cleaned shrimp ~ 3 min. later check for doneness. Drain & chill shrimp. ♥

There are 2 ways of spreading light — to be the candle or the mirror that reflects it.
♥ Edith Wharton

pure ORGANIC VITALITY
THE SPROUT GARDEN

Fresh organic produce counter; start on Sunday, Crisp & crunchy, they're when it's hard to grow pound, sprouts are a example: broccoli sprouts fighting sulforaphane broccoli — they're con- And so easy to grow. are available at health broccoli seeds, try radish, seeds; lentils, mung or Tbsp. seeds or beans jar. Cut a piece of jar opening & secure Cover seeds w/cold overnight. Drain & on its side & rinse each day. They'll grow sun can dry & overheat

grown right on your kitchen harvest on Wednesday. most valuable in winter fresh food outside. Pound for very big bang for the buck. For contain 20 times the tumor- glucosinolate (SGA) as mature centrated antioxidants! Viable, untreated seeds food stores. Besides cauliflower, or alfalfa azuki beans. Put 2-3 in a clean mayonnaise cheesecloth to fit over the it with a rubber band. water & let them sit rinse them — lay jar sprouts thoroughly twice in any light, but full them. Temperature

should be above 55° & below 75°. When they're looking sprouty, put them in the fridge but continue to rinse daily for freshness. Use them in salads & omelets, on sandwiches, or as garnish for veggies.

AZUKI

RADISH

LENTILS

TAKE TIME TO STOP & EAT THE FLOWERS

HEALTHY SALAD TOPPERS

Look at this page when you're making a salad to see what exciting little things you have on hand to spice things up 'cuz variety is the spice of life ♥.

Try lots of chopped Fresh Herbs, ♥ SPROUTS, Lemon, Orange & Lime Zest, ♥ coarsely ground Black Peppercorns ♥ Croutons (made from pita bread or bagels p. 69) ♥ Walnuts, Pine Nuts, or dry-roasted Peanuts ♥ Apple chunks, Pomegranate Seeds, Orange slices, ♥ dried Cherries, Cranberries, Blueberries, ♥ Fresh Flowers and flower petals, (Nasturtiums, Johnny Jump-Ups, Pansies) ♥ crumbled Blue Cheese, Feta, Goat Cheese, & Parmesan. Don't forget Avocadoes, Beets, hot, cooked Mushrooms, grated Carrots, Jicama, leftover Potatoes.

I worry about scientists discovering that lettuce has been fattening all along. ♥ Erma Bombeck

Broccoli Salad

156 CALORIES · 6 G. FAT · 162 MG. SODIUM · 9 G. PROTEIN · 19 G. CARBO · 3 G. FIBER

Serves 6

I often have a little bowl of this in the refrigerator. It's the perfect thing for when you open the fridge & just need to eat 3 bites of something! Crunchy!

1 lb. broccoli, in bite-sized pieces (raw)
½ c. raisins
¼ lb. mozzarella (part skim milk) in ½" dice
½ small red onion, thinly sliced, then chopped
1 tsp. lemon zest
1½ Tbsp. balsamic vinegar
¼ c. low-fat sour cream
3 Tbsp. low-fat mayonnaise

Put the broccoli, raisins, & cheese in a bowl. In another bowl combine all remaining ingred. & mix well. Pour over broccoli & toss. Serve chilled.

It takes 6 months to get into shape & 2 weeks to get out of shape. Once you know this you can stop being angry about other things in life & only be angry about this.
♥ Rita Rudner

JEI'S FAMOUS
CUCUMBER SALAD

66 CAL · 3 G. FAT · 2 G. PROTEIN · 7 G. CARBO · 2 G. FIBER · 188 MG. SODIUM

6 SERVINGS

I C Y & S P I C Y

2 Tbsp. Korean Hot Pepper Paste   2 green onions, minced
(Gourmet & Korean food stores)   1 Tbsp. ginger, minced
1 Tbsp. sesame oil   2 lg. cucumbers, peeled
1 ½ Tbsp. cider vinegar   ½ tsp. roasted sesame seeds

Mix together first 5 ingred. Slice cucumbers down the middle lengthwise & scoop out seeds w/ spoon ~ discard. Cut cukes into thin slices ~ mix w/ sauce & sprinkle over sesame seeds. Chill ½ hr.; stir & serve. ♥

CALAMARI SALAD

205 CAL · 7 G. FAT · 24 G. PROTEIN · 12 G. CARBO · 1 G. FIBER · 448 MG. SODIUM   Serves 6

F R E S H , C L E A N P R O T E I N

2 lb. calamari, cleaned   1 Tbsp. minced lime zest
¼ c. minced red pepper   2 Tbsp. chopped fresh cilantro,
¼ c. minced celery   or parsley
2 Tbsp. olive oil   ¼ tsp. Tabasco
½ c. fresh lime juice   ½ tsp. salt
2 Tbsp. orange marmalade   freshly ground pepper

Slice calamari into ¼" rings. Plunge into rapidly boiling water for 30 seconds ONLY. Drain, refresh in cold water. Put them in a bowl w/ red pepper & celery. Combine all other ingred. & pour over calamari. Chill well. ♥

IF & WHEN WERE PLANTED & NOTHING GREW. ♥

THIS BUD'S FOR YOU

FROZEN FLOWER BOWL

This just screams "Girl Party" — an ice bowl decorated with flowers & herbs & filled with the fruit of the season. Perfect for showers, lunches, birthdays — even brunch.

THE LITTLE THINGS THAT MAKE LIFE SWEET

AND NEITHER ARE THEY SOLD.

ARE WORTH THEIR WEIGHT IN GOLD;

THEY CAN'T BE BOUGHT AT ANY PRICE

To make the bowl: clean out a spot in your freezer (GOOD LUCK). Fill a bowl part way with water; drop in a cup or so of fresh flower blossoms, herbs, berries, or leaves. Put a smaller bowl in the big bowl & fill the little bowl with ice cubes to weigh it down. Cover the whole thing with a clean dish towel & tie it all up with string (to keep bowls in place as water expands). Freeze overnight. 20 min. before serving remove from freezer, unwrap & allow to sit at room temp. Separate bowls & fill with chilled fruit ~ drizzle Orange Dressing over all & toss gently. Set ice bowl in shallow dish & serve.

Orange Dressing: 3/4 c. fresh orange juice
1 Hbsp. o.j. frozen concentrate   1 Hbsp. orange zest
Combine dressing ingred. in a small saucepan; simmer; reduce to ½ c. Remove from heat & chill.

FRUIT SALADS

Summer Favorite
WATERMELON BALLS
BLUEBERRIES
STRAWBERRIES
CANTALOUPE BALLS
RED GRAPES
MANGO CHUNKS
MINT SPRIGS

Autumn Favorite
PEARS
POMEGRANATE SEEDS
GREEN GRAPES
TOASTED WALNUTS
THIN ICED RINGS OF RED ONION
DRY CRUMBLED BLUE CHEESE
Use autumn leaves for bowl.

Tropical Favorite
BANANA SLICES
PINEAPPLE CHUNKS
KIWI FRUIT
MANGO
STAR FRUIT
SHREDDED COCONUT
CHOPPED MACADAMIA NUTS

about — no matter what 'twas . . . You see, when you're hunting

82 CALORIES · 3 G. FAT · 1 G. PROTEIN

8 MG. SODIUM · 15 G. CARBOHYDRATE

BLUEBERRY SALAD

1 pint fresh blueberries
1 med. jicama, peeled & julienned
2 Tbsp. ginger, finely minced
1/4 c. mint leaves, slivered
1 Tbsp. olive oil
4 Tbsp. balsamic vinegar
1 Tbsp. orange juice concentrate
2 tsp. honey
radicchio leaves

Wash & pick over blueberries & put them in a bowl. Add the jicama, ginger, & mint. Combine oil, vinegar, frozen o.j., & honey in a jar & shake well. Pour over blueberries & toss gently. Arrange radicchio on plates & pile on the blueberries.

The game was to just find something about everything to be glad

for the glad things, you sort of forget the other kind. ♥ POLLYANNA

SPICY
MANGO SALAD

117 CAL · 1.4 G. FAT · 271 MG. SODIUM · 2 G. PROTEIN · 28 G. CARBO. 5 G. FIBER

Serves Six

I figure if I get **ONE** truly great, forever-in-my-life recipe out of a cookbook, I've got my money's worth. This is definitely one of those recipes. Serve it with everything!

1/4 c. fresh lime juice
1 Tbsp. light soy sauce
1 tsp. sesame oil
1 Tbsp. sugar
1 tsp. crushed red pepper
1/4 tsp. salt

3 mangoes, firm but ripe, peeled, julienned (1" long)
1 c. fresh blueberries
1 lg. red pepper, thinly julienned
1/2 c. red onion, finely chopped
1/2 c. cilantro leaves, chopped
1/2 c. fresh mint, chopped

Combine first 6 ingred. in a large bowl & whisk until sugar is dissolved. To the bowl, add remaining ingred. but don't toss until an hour before serving. Keep chilled.

My family is bilingual. We speak 2 languages. Unfortunately our 2nd language is Arg & Argy. My mother learned it from the funny papers — it was Little Orphan Annie's secret language. She taught it to my dad & they used it to speak privately in front of us kids (Christmas, polio shots, etc.). Like any children exposed to a "foreign" language, we learned it just by hearing it & now we're fluent. It HAS come in handy — I taught it to my best friends & we found a myriad of uses for it. It was best around boys! I would rather have had French but margy margotharger dargidargint sgargeek Fargrench—!

"When you see persons slip down on the ice, do not laugh at them.... It is more feminine on witnessing such a sight, to utter an involuntary scream." Eliza Leslie, Miss Leslie's Behavior Book 1859

ASIAN CHICKEN SALAD

WELCOME TO YOUR NEW ADDICTION ♥.

269 CAL · 8 G. FAT · 27 G. PROTEIN · 188 MG. SODIUM · 29 G. CARBO · 9 G. FIBER
Serves 6

1 lb. chicken breasts, skinned & boned
2 c. iceberg lettuce, thinly sliced
1 1/2 c. red cabbage, "   "
1 c. bean sprouts
3/4 c. cucumber, julienned
2 med. tomatoes, chopped
1 med. carrot, grated

3 green onions, chopped
1/4 c. fresh mint, chopped
1/4 c. fresh basil, "
1/4 c. cilantro, "
4 oz. hearts of palm, 1/2" rounds
1/2 c. dry roasted peanuts, chopped

Place chicken breasts in a skillet with 1" water. Cover & simmer gently for 10 min. ~ or just till done inside. Remove from water, cool & slice. Chill till ready to serve. Meanwhile combine all other ingred. in a large bowl. Toss with chicken and ♥.

FIERY THAI DRESSING

65 CAL · 2 G. FAT · 11 G. CARBO · 138 MG. SODIUM   Serves 8

So good you might wish to utter an involuntary scream ♥!
Combine all ingred. in jar & shake well. (Save leftover.)

1/4 c. + 2 Tbsp. fresh lime juice
1 Tbsp. sesame oil
2 Tbsp. fish sauce
4 tsp. chili puree w/ garlic

1/4 c. brown sugar
4 cloves garlic, minced
1/4 c. fresh ginger, minced
1/4 c. water
1/2 tsp. salt

"We did then what we knew how to do. Now that we know better, we do better."
♥ Oprah Winfrey talking to Maya Angelou on T.V.

CHICKEN & QUINOA SALAD

336 CALORIES · 9 G. FAT ·
22 G. PROTEIN · 5 G. FIBER

with PEANUTS, GINGER, & LIME

200 MG. SODIUM · 44 G. CARBO.
SERVES 6

4 chicken breasts, skinless, boneless; shredded

2 c. quinoa (AVAILABLE AT HEALTH FOOD STORES & SOME MARKETS)

4½ Tbsp. rice vinegar

1½ Tbsp. sesame oil

1½ tsp. low-sodium soy sauce

zest & juice from 2 juicy limes

3 Tbsp. fresh ginger, minced

¼ tsp. salt

1 c. snowpeas, trimmed & halved

¾ c. celery, chopped

¾ c. waterchestnuts, halved

5 green onions, chopped

½ c. currants

⅓ c. dry roasted unsalted peanuts, coarsely chopped

a few good grinds of black pepper, to taste

QUINOA

(ki-NOH-a)
IS A GRAIN THAT HAS 700% MORE IRON THAN ENRICHED WHITE RICE. EXCELLENT SOURCE OF PROTEIN & CALCIUM. COOKS FASTER THAN RICE. GREAT SOURCE OF FIBER. OH YEAH, TASTES GOOD TOO.☺!

Put 1" water in large skillet, simmer chicken breasts, covered, until just done. Remove from water & shred or chop. Set aside. Bring 3 c. water to boil in saucepan. Add quinoa. Bring back to boil, reduce to simmer, cover & steam 10 min. till tender. Strain & set aside. Meanwhile in a lg. bowl, mix all other ingred. Add chicken & quinoa. Stir well & serve.

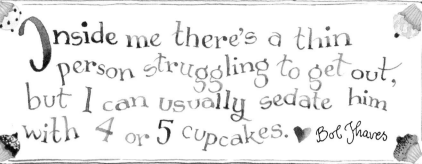

Inside me there's a thin person struggling to get out, but I can usually sedate him with 4 or 5 cupcakes. ♥ Bob Thaves

PORTION CONTROL

SERVING SIZES CAN BE CONFUSING, SO WHEN YOU HEAR THAT YOU SHOULD HAVE 2-3 "SERVINGS" OF CERTAIN FOODS EACH DAY, HERE'S WHAT IT MEANS:

A 3 OZ. SERVING OF FISH OR MEAT IS THE SIZE OF A DECK OF CARDS.

A SERVING SIZE OF FRUIT IS THE SIZE OF A TENNIS BALL.

↓ SHOP FOR THE SMALLER PORTIONS. ↓

½ CUP = 1 SERVING VEGETABLE

A LITTLE PAIR OF DICE EQUALS ONE OZ. CHEESE

A "MED." BAKED POTATO IS ABOUT THE SAME SIZE AS A COMPUTER MOUSE.

THINK A WEIGHT LOSS OF ¼ lb. ISN'T MUCH? IMAGINE A STICK-OF-BUTTER-SIZED-BIT OFF YOU!

A 1-lb.-A-WEEK WEIGHT LOSS IS SAFE & EASY & MORE LIKELY TO STAY OFF. ♥ AND, IN ONE YEAR, THAT'S 52 lbs !

BUT WHO'S COUNTING? ☺

GENERAL DAILY NUTRITION GUIDE

CALORIE REQUIREMENTS VARY ACCORDING TO SIZE, WEIGHT & ACTIVITY LEVEL

FOR WOMEN

	AGE 25-50	50+
CALORIES	2000	2000 or less
PROTEIN	50g	50g or less
FAT	65g or less	65g or less
SAT. FAT	22g or less	22g or less
CARBOS	300g	300g
FIBER	25-35g	25-35g
CHOLESTEROL	300mg or less	300mg or less
IRON	15mg	10mg
SODIUM	2400mg or less	2400mg or less
CALCIUM	1000mg	1200mg

H A L T

WE ARE MOST VULNERABLE WHEN WE ARE HUNGRY, ANGRY, LONELY, OR TIRED. JUST REMEMBER H.A.L.T. & TAKE C.A.R.E. ♥

H A L T

Only Irish coffee provides in a single glass all four essential food groups: alcohol, sugar, caffeine & fat. ♥ Alex Levine

CHICKEN STOCK

Deep, dark & delicious ~ full of vitamins & low-fat but so rich in flavor, it makes unbelievable soups, sauces & gravy. It bubbles for hours so start a pot the first chilly morning when the leaves start falling.

1 6~7 lb. whole chicken
1 c. white wine
3 carrots, unpeeled, in 2" pieces
3 celery stalks w/ leaves, in 2" pieces
2 med. onions w/ skin, quartered
a handful of fresh parsley
½ Tbsp. whole black peppercorns
2 bay leaves

Wash chicken, discard liver. Rinse giblets & neck, dry them & whack them into 1" pieces with a big knife. Put them in a large soup pot with about a Tbsp. of olive oil over high heat. Add 1 onion (quartered). Stir & cook for about 15-20 min. till everything, including bottom of pan, is dark brown. Add white wine & deglaze by scraping up all the brown bits from the bottom of the pan. Add rest of ingred. including chicken; cover everything with cold water, bring to boil. Set lid on slightly askew & simmer 1½~2 hrs. till chicken is just done. Remove chicken from pot & cool. Pick off meat & set aside. Put all skin & bones back into soup pot & continue simmering for 4-5 hrs. Strain & refrigerate uncovered overnight. Scrape congealed fat off top & discard. Make stock richer for gravy & sauces by boiling it down ~ or stretch it further with white wine or canned chicken broth. Freeze some in ice cube trays for little servings.

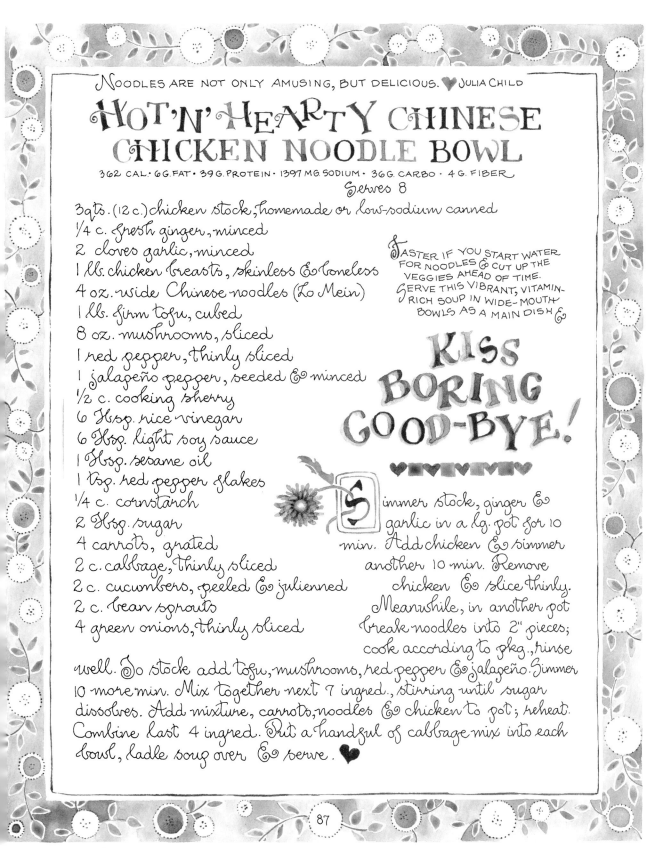

NOODLES ARE NOT ONLY AMUSING, BUT DELICIOUS. ♥ JULIA CHILD

HOT 'N' HEARTY CHINESE CHICKEN NOODLE BOWL

362 CAL. • 6 G. FAT • 39 G. PROTEIN • 1397 MG. SODIUM • 36 G. CARBO • 4 G. FIBER

Serves 8

3 qts. (12 c.) chicken stock, homemade or low-sodium canned
1/4 c. fresh ginger, minced
2 cloves garlic, minced
1 lb. chicken breasts, skinless & boneless
4 oz. wide Chinese noodles (Lo Mein)
1 lb. firm tofu, cubed
8 oz. mushrooms, sliced
1 red pepper, thinly sliced
1 jalapeño pepper, seeded & minced
1/2 c. cooking sherry
6 Tbsp. rice vinegar
6 Tbsp. light soy sauce
1 Tbsp. sesame oil
1 tsp. red pepper flakes
1/4 c. cornstarch
2 Tbsp. sugar
4 carrots, grated
2 c. cabbage, thinly sliced
2 c. cucumbers, peeled & julienned
2 c. bean sprouts
4 green onions, thinly sliced

FASTER IF YOU START WATER FOR NOODLES & CUT UP THE VEGGIES AHEAD OF TIME. SERVE THIS VIBRANT, VITAMIN-RICH SOUP IN WIDE-MOUTH BOWLS AS A MAIN DISH &

KISS BORING GOOD-BYE!

♥♥♥♥♥♥♥♥

Simmer stock, ginger & garlic in a lg. pot for 10 min. Add chicken & simmer another 10 min. Remove chicken & slice thinly. Meanwhile, in another pot break noodles into 2" pieces; cook according to pkg., rinse well. To stock add tofu, mushrooms, red pepper & jalapeño. Simmer 10 more min. Mix together next 7 ingred., stirring until sugar dissolves. Add mixture, carrots, noodles & chicken to pot; reheat. Combine last 4 ingred. Put a handful of cabbage mix into each bowl, ladle soup over & serve. ♥

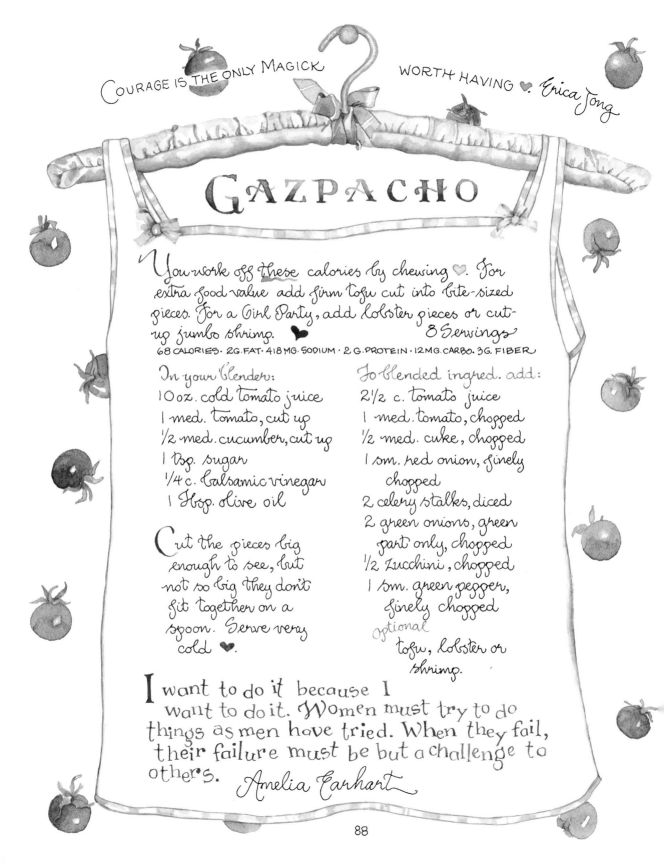

GAZPACHO

You work off these calories by chewing ♥. For extra food value add firm tofu cut into bite-sized pieces. For a Girl Party, add lobster pieces or cut-up jumbo shrimp. ♥   8 Servings

68 CALORIES · 2G. FAT · 418 MG. SODIUM · 2 G. PROTEIN · 12 MG. CARBO. 3G. FIBER

In your blender:
10 oz. cold tomato juice
1 med. tomato, cut up
½ med. cucumber, cut up
1 tsp. sugar
¼ c. balsamic vinegar
1 tbsp. olive oil

Cut the pieces big enough to see, but not so big they don't fit together on a spoon. Serve very cold ♥.

To blended ingred. add:
2½ c. tomato juice
1 med. tomato, chopped
½ med. cuke, chopped
1 sm. red onion, finely chopped
2 celery stalks, diced
2 green onions, green part only, chopped
½ zucchini, chopped
1 sm. green pepper, finely chopped
optional
    tofu, lobster or shrimp.

I want to do it because I want to do it. Women must try to do things as men have tried. When they fail, their failure must be but a challenge to others. *Amelia Earhart*

88

COUNTRY BOUILLABAISSE
WITH FRESH HERBS

401 CAL. • 6 G.FAT • 43 G.PROTEIN • 788 MG. SODIUM • 31 G. CARBO. • 5 G. FIBER

Serves Six

This is a sensual dish ~ for the full experience serve it with a a basket of Garlicky Bagel Toasts (p. 69), steamed artichokes drizzled w/ lemon juice, & fresh strawberries for dessert. ♥

2 tsp. olive oil
6 cloves garlic, minced
2 lbs. onion, chopped
28 oz. can tomatoes
8 oz. bottled clam juice
2 c. good white wine
3/4 c. fresh parsley, chopped
1 tsp. dried thyme
3 bay leaves
1/4 tsp. crushed red pepper

salt & pepper, to taste
18 littleneck clams, scrubbed
18 mussels, scrubbed & debearded
18 lg. shrimp, peeled & deveined
1/2 lb. bass, monkfish, or cod (in chunks)
1/2 lbs. scallops
1/4 c. fresh basil, chopped

Heat oil in a lg. soup pot & sauté garlic & onions slowly till soft. Add next 7 ingred. & simmer 20 min. Taste & add salt & freshly ground pepper. Use right away, chill, or freeze. Final cooking: To hot soup add clams & mussels; cover & simmer 5 min. Add remaining seafood, cover & cook another 3~4 min. just till shrimp are cooked through & shellfish is open. Remove bay leaves & any shellfish that didn't open as you serve in large wide-mouthed soup bowls. ♥ Splurges: lobster or crabs. (I almost forgot ~ stir basil into soup just before serving!)

"I MAY NOT KNOW MUCH" ⎯ ANOTHER FORM OF LOCUTION OFTEN FAVORED BY HER. THE TONE IN WHICH IT WAS SPOKEN UTTERLY BELIED THE WORDS; THE TONE TOLD YOU THAT NOT ONLY DID SHE KNOW MUCH, BUT ALL.

♥ Edna Ferber

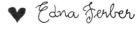

"HOW LONG DOES GETTING THIN TAKE?" ASKED POOH ANXIOUSLY. ♥ A.A. MILNE

MARVELOUS
Mushroom Soup

148 CAL. • 3 G. FAT • 12 G. PROTEIN • 827 MG. SODIUM • 19 G. CARBO. • 4 G. FIBER

Makes 8 Servings

3 med. onions, peeled & thinly sliced
1 Tbsp. olive oil
1 clove garlic, minced
6 c. chicken stock, homemade (p. 86) or canned SALT FREE
1 lb. mushrooms, mixed, shiitake & baby bell, or?
¼ c. tomato paste
¼ c. white port
1½ tsp. salt
½ tsp. freshly ground pepper
1 tsp. Parmesan cheese per serving

Slice onions very thinly & sauté in olive oil for about 1 hr. — add garlic about halfway through & continue cooking until slightly caramelized & very soft. Add stock, sliced mushrooms & all other ingred. except cheese. Simmer gently for ½ hr. Serve w/ Parmesan & Garlicky Bagel Toasts (p. 69). ♥

EAT AS MUCH AS YOU LIKE — JUST DON'T SWALLOW IT.
♥ STEVE BURNS

THE BEST THINGS IN LIFE AREN'T THINGS. ♡

VIBRANT VEGGIES

BRUSSELS SPROUTS: Wash them & pull off tough outer leaves; cut an X in the bottom of each & cook till tender. Toss w/ a little olive oil, s. & p., & freshly grated nutmeg. ♡

CARROTS: Sauté grated carrots in a little olive oil, some o.j., a few golden raisins, & some minced fresh ginger. ♥

ROASTED ASPARAGUS: Preheat oven to 500°. Snap off bottoms of asparagus ~ put them in a single layer on an olive-oil-sprayed baking sheet & spray them lightly. Cook 8-10 min. till tender; sprinkle w/ salt & freshly ground pepper & serve. ♥

GREEN BEANS & ALMONDS: Steam beans till tender. Meanwhile sauté slivered almonds in olive oil ~ toss w/ beans, s. & p., & a squeeze of lemon juice. Serve. ♥

CHERRY TOMATOES: Sauté shallots & garlic in olive oil till softened. Add in halved & quartered cherry tomatoes. Heat until warmed through ~ 2 min., remove from heat ~ sprinkle over fresh parsley, basil, & salt & pepper. Serve. ♥

CRISPED MUSHROOMS: You need a seasoned iron pan for this. Put it over high heat DRY. Drop in THINLY sliced mushrooms; keep tossing. Mushrooms will give up their liquid & it will evaporate. Mushrooms are fabulous hot, over salads, other veggies, & w/ fish & meat. ♥

FOOD IS AN IMPORTANT PART OF A BALANCED DIET. ♥ Fran Lebowitz

ONION FLOWERS

115 CAL · 3 G. FAT · 3 G. PROTEIN
348 MG. SODIUM · 20 G. CARBO · 4 G. FIBER
per person   400°

Onions are so good for you & this recipe makes them sweet as pie. ♥

Preheat oven to 400°. Peel onion. Scoop out the center w/ the large end of a melon baller. With a sharp knife crosshatch the onion ⊞ 1/3 of the way down from the top. Set onion on a piece of aluminum foil ~ stuff cavity with all remaining ingred. Wrap it in foil; bake 1¼ hrs. ♥

1 med. onion, Vidalia
or Spanish
1 clove garlic, peeled
½ tsp. chicken base
½ tsp. Parmesan cheese
½ tsp. olive oil
salt & pepper, to taste

NOTE: CHICKEN BASE, IN OUR MKT., COMES IN A JAR LABELED "BETTER THAN BOUILLON" ~ HEAVEN, HANDY STUFF ~ CONCENTRATED CHICKEN FLAVOR. IT'S WET, YOU SPOON IT OUT LIKE APPLESAUCE.

LEMON ARTICHOKES

100 CAL. · 2 G. FAT · 5 G. PROTEIN · 685 MG. SODIUM · 18 G. CARBO · 9 G. FIBER
PER PERSON

Keep some in the fridge ~ they're delicious hot or cold. ♥

Wash & trim artichokes; put them in a lg. pot w/ just enough cold water to cover. Add oil, salt & lots of pepper. Cover; boil, then simmer gently until fork pierces stem easily. Drain. Squeeze lemon juice over.

1 lg. artichoke per person
1-2 Tbsp. olive oil
1 tsp. salt
freshly cracked pepper
fresh lemon juice

IF YOU DON'T WANT YOUR CHILDREN TO HEAR WHAT YOU'RE SAYING, PRETEND YOU'RE TALKING TO THEM. ♥ ANON:

BOURBON-MASHED SWEET POTATOES

260 CALORIES · 0.7 G. FAT · 30 MG. SODIUM · 3.5 G. PROTEIN
58 G. CARBS · 6 G. FIBER   450° SERVES 8

This is fabulous served with the Crusted Baked Cod on p. 105 or roast chicken or for any fall or winter comfort-food dinner. ♥

ORANGE VEGETABLES (THE DARKER THE BETTER) ARE HIGH IN BETA CAROTENE

5 lbs. (about 8 med.) sweet potatoes or yams
1/4 c. bourbon
1/4 c. brown sugar
zest of 1/2 lemon
1 tbsp. lemon juice
salt & freshly ground pepper to taste

Preheat oven to 450°. Pierce potatoes with a knife a few times & bake 1 hr. until soft. Let cool 15 min. Halve potatoes & scoop pulp into a large mixing bowl. Partially mash; add all other ingred. & mash well & serve. ♥

Bow down to her on Sunday
Salute her when her birthday comes
♥ Bob Dylan

"It's been about 2 months since Shana left & I have yet to make any poor decisions regarding women and/or dating. I'm on a roll. Now if I can just get that mantra down that you assured me would work the next time around: Just do what the woman wants... Just do what the woman wants.. Just do what the woman wants..."

♥ EXCERPT FROM MY EX-HUSBAND'S LETTER

WHITE RICE with COCONUT & LIME

268 CALORIES · 6 G. FAT · 51 G. CARBO.   6 SERVINGS

2 3/4 c. chicken broth
2 c. white rice
1/2 c. dried, unsweetened coconut
1/3 c. fresh mint, chopped
2 tbsp. cilantro, chopped
zest of one lime
juice of one lime

Preheat oven to 350°. In a large saucepan bring chicken broth & rice to boil. Stir, cover, reduce heat to low & cook 15-20 min. (till liquid has been absorbed). Meanwhile, toast coconut on cookie sheet in oven for 7-10 min., until golden. Remove rice from heat, stir in coconut & all other ingred. Serve. ♥

SOME CENSURING READERS WILL SCORNFULLY SAY, WHY HATH THIS LADY WRIT HER OWN LIFE? SINCE NONE CARES TO KNOW WHOSE DAUGHTER SHE WAS OR WHOSE WIFE SHE IS, OR HOW SHE WAS BRED, OR WHAT FORTUNES SHE HAD, OR HOW SHE LIVED, OR WHAT HUMOR OR DISPOSITION SHE WAS OF? I ANSWER THAT IT IS TRUE, THAT 'TIS TO NO PURPOSE TO THE READERS, BUT IT IS TO THE AUTHORESS, BECAUSE I WRITE IT FOR MY OWN SAKE, NOT THEIRS.
♥ Margaret Cavendish in 1655

GARLIC
MASHED POTATOES

106 CALORIES • 0.5 G. FAT • 55 MG. SODIUM • 3.9 G. PROTEIN • 22 G. CARBO • 1.7G. FIBER

Serves 8

You'll never need butter again !

10 med. baking potatoes
peeled & halved
10 whole cloves garlic, peeled

1½ c. buttermilk
salt & pepper to taste

Drop potatoes & garlic into a large pot of boiling water & cook until potatoes are fork tender. Drain & mash in a large bowl with buttermilk & salt & pepper. Serve. ♥ (yes, mash the garlic in with potatoes!)

POTATO PANCAKES
PURE COMFORT FOOD

yum
yum
yum

Preheat oven to 450°
Spray a cookie sheet with oil. Form leftover potatoes into patties. Bake 20 min., turning once, until golden. ♥

"IT ALL COMES," SAID POOH CROSSLY, "OF NOT HAVING FRONT DOORS BIG ENOUGH." "IT ALL COMES," SAID RABBIT STERNLY, "OF EATING TOO MUCH. I THOUGHT AT THE TIME," SAID RABBIT, "ONLY I DIDN'T LIKE TO SAY ANYTHING," SAID RABBIT, "THAT ONE OF US WAS EATING TOO MUCH," SAID RABBIT, AND I KNEW IT WASN'T ME," HE SAID." ♥ A.A.MILNE

Bird Nests

227 CAL. · 12 G. FAT · 22 G. PROTEIN · 648 MG. SODIUM · 8 G. CARBO · 2 G. FIBER

Serves 6

Turkey rolled into crisp lettuce packages ~ deliciously sloppy & fun to eat. ♥

- 1 head of iceberg lettuce

	DIPPING SAUCE
½ c. rice wine vinegar	
1½ Tbsp. light soy sauce	
1 tsp. sesame oil	
1 dash Tabasco sauce	

- 2 tsp. olive oil
- 1½ lb. ground turkey breast
- 1 c. red pepper, finely chopped
- ½ tsp. salt
- freshly ground pepper to taste
- 2½ Tbsp. fresh ginger, minced
- 2 Tbsp. light soy sauce
- 2 Tbsp. fresh lime juice
- 4 green onions, chopped
- ⅓ c. peanuts, chopped (opt.: THEY ADD 4 G. FAT PER SERVING – BUT GOOD FOR YOU!)

Separate iceberg lettuce into whole leaves & refrigerate. Mix together next 4 ingred. in a small bowl & set aside. Heat oil in skillet, add turkey, red pepper, S & P. Cook 4 min. till meat is no longer pink, breaking up pieces as you stir. Add ginger, soy sauce, & lime juice ~ cook for another minute. Just before serving, stir in green onions & peanuts. To serve, put ¼ c. turkey in each lettuce leaf, roll up into little packages & serve with dipping sauce. ♥

Treetalk and
Windsong are
the language of
my mother —
her music does
not leave me.
BARBARA MAHONE

COLD ROLLS

WITH PEANUTS: 326 CAL. · 12 G. FAT · 10 G. PROTEIN · 49 G. CARBO · 209 MG. SODIUM · 4 G. FIBER
WITHOUT PEANUTS: 255 CAL. · 6 G. FAT · 7 G. PROTEIN · 46 G. CARBO · 110 MG. SODIUM · 3 G. FIBER
(THESE NUMBERS INCLUDE SAUCE.)

Serves 6 (makes 12 rolls)

The most perfect of lunches. Make a batch on Sunday & eat all week.

1 c. soaked bean threads (thin rice noodles)
1 c. iceberg lettuce in 1" matchstick
3/4 c. cucumber in 1" matchstick
3/4 c. bean sprouts
3/4 c. firm tofu, cut in strips
1/4 c. salted peanuts, coarsely chopped (GO WILD, HAVE THEM!)

1 med. carrot, peeled & grated
1 1/2 Tbsp. fresh ginger, minced
2 Tbsp. fresh mint, chopped
2 Tbsp. fresh basil, "
2 Tbsp. cilantro, "
12 rice paper rounds or spring roll skins (NOT eggroll wraps)

RICE PAPER ROUNDS ARE THIN WHITE DISKS, CRISP UNTIL SOAKED. IF YOU CAN'T FIND THEM OR THE BEAN THREADS CALL DEAN & DELUCA IN N.Y. 1-800-999-0306 & THEY'LL SEND THEM. ♥

Soak bean threads in a bowl of hot water 15 min. till soft; drain & cut into 3" lengths; combine in a lg. bowl with all other ingred. (except rice paper rounds). Prepare a stack of 12 single sheets of paper towels. Fill a wide bowl or plate w/ HOT water & soak a rice paper round until soft ~ 2-3 min. Carefully place on paper towel. Put 1/2 c. filling in bottom 3rd of round & roll up as tightly as possible, turning sides in to enclose as you roll. To keep: wrap them in damp paper towels (keeps skins from drying out) & then, by 2, into plastic baggies & into fridge. Serve with:

COLD ROLL SAUCE

1/4 c. sugar
1/2 c. water
1/4 c. red wine vinegar
1/4 c. rice wine vinegar
2 Tbsp. fish sauce
1 tsp. jalapeño, seeded & minced

1 tsp. fresh ginger, minced
1/2 carrot, peeled & grated
1 green onion, chopped
2 Tbsp. lime juice
pinch cayenne

Bring sugar & water to boil in a small sauce pan. Lower heat & simmer 10 min. Add remaining ingred. & chill. ♥

ROAST TURKEY

I'm really not that good in the kitchen. I use the smoke alarm as a timer.
♥ NATHAN HALE

247 CAL · 5 G. FAT · 27 G. PROTEIN · 13 G. CARBO. · 230 MG. SODIUM · 2 G. FIBER

375° 6 Servings

So nice after a hard day ~ full of delicious L-Tryptophan, a natural mood elevator & appetite suppressor (among other things). This is simple, solid "diet" food. ♥ GOES TOGETHER QUICKLY ♥

1 3 lb. turkey breast	2 cloves garlic, chopped
1 c. fat-free, low-salt chicken broth	1 Tbsp. ginger, minced
1 c. dry white wine	1 tsp. dried thyme
1 Tbsp. fresh lime juice	½ tsp. salt
2 lg. carrots, cut in 3" sticks	½ c. golden raisins
2 med. onions, sliced	2 Tbsp. minced parsley
	freshly ground pepper

Preheat oven to 375°. Place washed & dried breast in 9"x13"(ish) roasting pan. Pour in broth, wine, & lime juice. Surround with carrots, onion, garlic, ginger, thyme & salt. Stir around the edges a bit. Pop into oven, uncovered & bake for 2 hrs. (or until the little button pops up). Baste turkey & veg every ½ hr. with pan juices. Add raisins for last 15 min. of cooking. When done, remove skin, sprinkle over parsley & freshly ground pepper. Serve sliced w/ a little pile of onions, some carrot & raisins & pan juices. ♥ P.S. L-Tryptophan is also famous for making people sleep like babies. ♥

SPIRITUAL LOVE IS A POSITION OF STANDING WITH ONE HAND EXTENDED INTO THE UNIVERSE & ONE HAND EXTENDED INTO THE WORLD, LETTING OURSELVES BE A CONDUIT FOR PASSING ENERGY.
♥ CHRISTINA BALDWIN

SHRIMP & SPINACH
With Linguini

314 CALORIES · 9 G. FAT · 28 G. PROTEIN · 29 G. CARB · 39 G. SODIUM

400° Serves 6

Chopped greens, mixed in with pasta, up the vitamins & up the crunch & just make the whole thing better. ♥

1½ lbs. lg. shrimp, peeled & deveined
1½ red bell pepper, seeded & thinly sliced
3 tbsp. olive oil
4 lg. cloves garlic, pressed
scant ½ tsp. red pepper flakes
¼ c. + 2 tbsp. fresh lime juice
½ tsp. salt
¼ c. + 2 tbsp. bottled clam juice
6 oz. linguini
6 c. fresh spinach, washed & dried; stems removed
Parmesan cheese (opt.)

Preheat oven to 400°. Put a large pot of water on to boil (for pasta). Wash & pat shrimp dry. Put them in a shallow baking dish along with the sliced peppers. Put olive oil into small pan over med. heat & add garlic, red pepper flakes, fresh lime juice & salt. Cook 4 min. stirring often. Pour over shrimp & peppers & stir gently. Spread shrimp & peppers evenly in dish & bake 15 min. Meanwhile cook linguini according to pkg. instructions. Tear spinach into bite-sized pieces. Drain & rinse pasta, PUT IN BOWL, pour shrimp over & toss gently. Add spinach, toss again & serve with Parmesan if you like. (Good cold too!)

The older you get, the harder it is to lose weight, because your body has made friends with your fat.
♥ Lynne Alpern & Esther Blumenfeld

SING: ♪ SHE'S VENUS IN BLUE JEANS, ♪ MONA LISA IN A PONYTAIL ... ♪

GRILLED *Spiced* SALMON
With Toasted Mushrooms

235 CAL • 6 G. FAT • 35 G PROTEIN • 10 G. CARBO • 116 MG SODIUM • 4 G. FIBER

Serves One

Do you have one of those little flat, ridged, cast-iron pans you use on top of your stove to grill on? They are really wonderful. ♥ This is the perfect little dinner ~ try it like this or serve the salmon with the Blueberry Salad on p.81 ♥.

1/3 lb. salmon fillet, skinned
2 tsp. spice rub (see below)
10 big mushrooms, thinly sliced
thinly sliced red onion

greens: spinach, romaine, or
   mesclun mix
lemon
nasturtium flowers (opt.)

Spray grill with olive oil; set over high heat until it begins to smoke. Rinse salmon, dry it & rub the spice rub all over it. Cook over high heat about 5 min., turn it, reduce heat & cook until fish is opaque inside. Meanwhile put a big iron frying pan (dry) over high heat & add mushrooms. Stir constantly till crisped ~ set aside. Arrange greens on a plate ~ sprinkle over onions, then mushrooms, then hot salmon. Squeeze lemon over ~ decorate with nasturtiums & serve. ♥

MIDDLE EAST SPICE RUB

Mix all ingred. together & keep a jarful around to rub flavor into fish, poultry, & meat. ♥

1/4 c. Lemon Pepper (from mkt.)
1/4 c. dried oregano
1/4 c. sesame seeds

2 Tbsp. paprika
1 Tbsp. garlic powder

GIVE SOME TO YOUR FRIEND ♥.

AVOCADO-KIWI Salsa

109 CAL · 8G. FAT · 11G. CARBO.
(PER SERVING) 6 SERVINGS

I got this recipe from a darling lady I met on the train going through the Rockies to California (where avocadoes grow on trees)♥. Quick & easy, it spruces up everything it touches (FOR EXAMPLE, SEE MENU, RIGHT↗). ♥

2 med. avocadoes
3 Tbsp. fresh lime juice
2 kiwis, peeled & cubed

ALSO GOOD W/ PINK GRAPEFRUIT OR MANGOES. ♥

1/4 c. red onion, finely chopped
2 Tbsp. red pepper,   "   "
3 Tbsp. cilantro, chopped
1/4 tsp. crushed red pepper
1/2 tsp. salt
freshly ground pepper, to taste

Cube avocadoes (see right) & scoop into bowl; pour over lime juice & toss gently. Peel & cube the kiwis; add them to avocadoes along with all remaining ingredients. Refrigerate till ready to use. ♥ (WE ALSO LOVED THIS ON CHICKEN.)

I don't have a fear of flying, I have a fear of landing too fast.
♥ Marty Ingalls

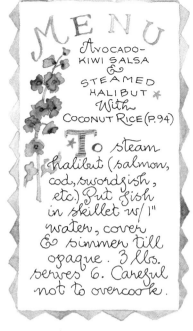

MENU
AVOCADO-KIWI SALSA & STEAMED HALIBUT * With COCONUT RICE (P.94)

To steam halibut (salmon, cod, swordfish, etc.) Put fish in skillet w/ 1" water, cover & simmer till opaque. 3 lbs. serves 6. Careful not to overcook.

GRAVITY: NOT ONLY A GOOD IDEA, IT'S THE LAW.

CUTTING

To cube an avocado, cut it in half lengthwise, remove seed. Score flesh through just to skin & scoop out with a large spoon.

AVOCADOES

PORK TENDERLOINS WITH APPLES & CIDER LENTILS

547 CAL. · 11G. FAT · 57G. PROTEIN · 463 MG. SODIUM · 57G. CARBO. · 20 G. FIBER

Serves 8

Only 2 Tbsp. added fat (olive oil) but it's a dinner you'd be proud to serve at any special occasion. Fun to cook: Put 2 lg. skillets & a lg. saucepan on top of the stove ~ make lentils first, start the pork, then the sauce.

CIDER LENTILS

1 lb. tiny black lentils
1½ c. water
1½ c. apple cider
2 tsp. chicken bouillon (paste)
3 whole cloves
2 bay leaves
1 sm. onion, minced
salt & pepper

Combine all ingred. (except s. & p.) in a lg. saucepan & bring to a boil. Reduce heat, cover & simmer 40-45 min. till liquid has been absorbed. S. & P. to taste ~ remove bay leaves.

Apple Sauce

1½ c. apple cider
½ tsp. cinnamon
3 green apples, peeled & sliced in ½" wedges
1½ Tbsp. minced fresh ginger
½ tsp. ground sage
3/4 c. dry white wine
3 c. chicken stock or broth
zest of 1 orange
1 tsp. arrowroot

PORK TENDERLOINS

3 lbs. pork tenderloins   2 Tbsp. olive oil
salt & pepper   4 or 5 lg. shallots,
                              peeled & halved

Pat pork dry, salt & pepper. In a lg. skillet over high heat, brown meat & shallots well on all sides. Cook until instant-read thermometer registers 150° in thickest part. Remove to serv. plate, cover w/ foil & let sit 10 min. before carving. (Save pan for finishing sauce.)

Put 3/4 c. cider, cinnamon & apples in lg. skillet, simmer 2-3 min. till apples are just soft, remove them from pan & set aside. Add in rest of cider. Remove browned shallots from pork pan; chop & add to cider w/ ginger, sage & wine. Boil 4 min. Add chicken stock, boil & reduce by half. Add zest, whisk in arrowroot. Pour off fat from pork pan; pour sauce into pan & scrape up any bits of meat ~ add in apples & reheat. Slice pork, arrange on plates w/ lentils, spoon sauce over pork & enjoy.

TURKEY MEATLOAF

287 CALORIES · 10.8 G. FAT · 645 MG. SODIUM · 21.6 G. PROTEIN · 26.3 G. CARB · 3.4 G. FIBER
375° SERVES 6

This is so delicious I sometimes mistake it for a snackin' cake! Keep in mind, one piece is low-fat & low calorie, however eating the whole thing is NOT. Serve with Garlic Mashed Potatoes (p. 95) & be glad you're alive. ∵

2 tsp. olive oil
1 c. finely chopped onion
1 c. finely chopped celery
1 c. finely diced carrot
1 c. chopped mushrooms
2 egg whites
1 Hsp. steak sauce (A-1 or Pickapeppa)

½ c. chopped green onion
½ c. catsup
2 Hsp. minced fresh parsley
1 tsp. dried thyme
½ tsp. salt
1 tsp. pepper
1 c. seasoned bread crumbs
1¼ lbs. ground turkey

Preheat oven to 375°. Put olive oil in lg. sauté pan over med. high heat; add onion, celery, carrot & mushrooms. Sauté 7 min. Remove from heat; set aside to cool. In a bowl mix together egg whites, steak sauce, green onion, catsup, parsley, thyme, salt & pepper. Add ground turkey, bread crumbs & cooled vegetables. Mix well & shape into a solid loaf in a sprayed baking pan. Bake 50 min. & serve ♥.

I HATE TO EAT AND EAT AND EAT AND RUN. ♥ NEILA ROSS

CHICKEN DINNER

557 CAL· 10G. FAT ·50 G. PROTEIN · 408 MG. SODIUM · 67G. CARBO · 9 G. FIBER

6 SERVINGS~ A LOWER FAT VERSION OF THE CLASSIC GOTTA-HAVE-IT, COMFORT-FOOD DINNER.

ROASTED VEGETABLES

spray olive oil

4 med. Idaho potatoes, not peeled, scrubbed & cut into wedges

5 lg. carrots, peeled & cut into uniform pieces

3 lg. parsnips, peeled & cut into pieces, like carrots

6 shallots, halved & peeled

3 heads garlic

If you'd rather not have potatoes ~ have green beans & mushrooms. Preheat oven to 475°. Spray lg. baking sheet w/oil. Cut veggies, put each group into a bowl, spray lightly & toss; arrange flat on pan. S & P. Roast 35 min. Meanwhile prepare garlic as on p. 72, & then chicken.

LEMON CHICKEN

4 lbs. roasting chicken

1 lemon

1 tsp. dried thyme

When veggies come out, set aside; reduce heat to 375°.

Wash & pat chicken dry ~ put in a large oil sprayed roasting pan. Cut lemon into 4 thick slices & slip them under skin next to breast meat ~ left over lemon goes inside cavity. Spray chicken with oil & sprinkle thyme all over. Put it & garlic heads in oven. (Make gravy.) After 1/2 hr. remove chicken from oven, baste w/pan juices, add roasted veggies to pan & continue to cook 35 min. more or until thigh juices run clear when deeply pierced. When done, let sit 10 min. Carve, discard lemons & skin. Surround chicken pieces with veggies & 1/2 head of roasted garlic each ~ pour gravy over all.

Wavy Gravy:
1 3/4 c. rich chicken stock (p. 86), or 1-14oz. can chicken broth; 1/4 c. dry white wine; 1 tsp. chicken base (bouillon paste); 1 tsp. arrowroot. Put 1st 3 ingred. in saucepan, boil & reduce by half. Whisk in arrowroot to thicken. S. and P. to taste.

My 10-YEAR-OLD DAUGHTER IS MY #1 POWER SOURCE.
♥ HANAN MIKHAIL ASHRAWI

CRUSTED BAKED COD

350° Serves 4

232 CAL · 4 G. FAT · 33 G. PROTEIN · 213 MG. SODIUM · 16 G. CARBO · 1 G. FIBER

Delicate, clean-tasting cod, crisped up in the oven.
Delicious w/ a green salad, or make it more with
Bourbon Mashed Sweet Potatoes (p. 93). ♥

½ c. bread crumbs
2 Tbsp. parsley, minced
1 Tbsp. green onion, minced
1 Tbsp. fresh ginger, minced (or 1 Tbsp. horseradish)
1 clove garlic, minced
zest of 1 lemon
2 Tbsp. sesame seeds
⅛ tsp. cayenne
spray olive oil
1½ lbs. cod or other whitefish
lemon wedges

Preheat oven to 350°. Combine 1st 8 ingred. Rinse
cod & pat dry; put into olive-oil-sprayed baking
dish. Spread topping over & spray lightly again.
Bake 25 min. Serve with lemon wedges. ♥

BROCCOLI LINGUINI WITH CLAM SAUCE

266 CAL. · 5 G. FAT · 10 G. PROTEIN · 485 MG. SODIUM · 38 G. CARBO · 3 G. FIBER

MAKES 6 BIG SERVINGS

All the satisfaction of pasta but by using less & replacing it with the versatile "broccoli slaw" now available in markets, it's all the better for YOU. ♥

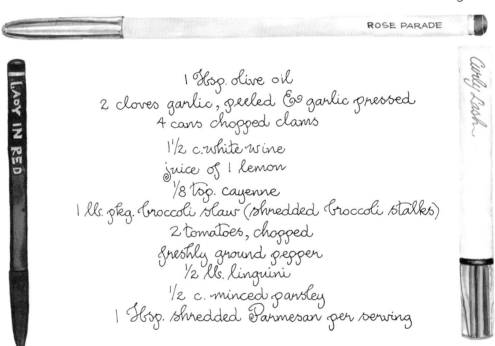

1 Tbsp. olive oil
2 cloves garlic, peeled & garlic pressed
4 cans chopped clams
1½ c. white wine
juice of 1 lemon
⅛ tsp. cayenne
1 lb. pkg. broccoli slaw (shredded broccoli stalks)
2 tomatoes, chopped
freshly ground pepper
½ lb. linguini
½ c. minced parsley
1 Tbsp. shredded Parmesan per serving

Bring a pot of water to boil for pasta. In another lg. saucepan heat oil & add garlic — when it's sizzling & barely turning color add the liquid from canned clams (reserve clams), wine, lemon & cayenne. Boil 10 min. Mean—while put broccoli & tomatoes into a lg. bowl. Cook pasta. Add reserved clams to clam juice & bring to boil. Rinse pasta in hot water & pour it over broccoli mix in bowl. Pour clam juice over all, toss well. Sprinkle on minced parsley. Pass the Parmesan. ♥

I believe in hard work. It keeps the wrinkles out of the mind & the spirit. ♥ Helena Rubinstein

"...I'M NOT AFRAID OF STORMS FOR I'M LEARNING HOW TO SAIL MY SHIP." ♥ LOUISA MAY ALCOTT

LOBSTER CAKES

270 CAL.·4 G.FAT·28 G.PROTEIN·965 MG.SODIUM·32 G.CARBO·3 G.FIBER

400°   Serves 4

2 c. cooked lobster meat, diced
(or cracked crab-meat)
1 egg white, beaten
1 dash worcestershire
1/4 c. flour
1 tsp. baking powder
2 tsp. onion, grated
2 Tbsp. parsley, minced
1/2 tsp. salt
1 pinch cayenne
1/2 c. bread crumbs (pref. homemade)
greens

Gently combine everything but bread crumbs & greens.
Make 4 patties, coat w/ bread crumbs & chill at least
1/2 hr. Preheat oven to 400°. Spray baking sheet with
olive oil, arrange patties on it & spray them lightly.
Bake for 15 min., turning once. Serve on a bed of
greens with Peach-Mango Mayo. ♥

Peach Mango Mayo

NUTRITIONAL ANALYSIS ABOVE INCLUDES MAYO

1 c. mango, diced
1 peach, peeled, diced
3 Tbsp. red pepper, minced
3 Tbsp. green pepper, "

2 Tbsp. shallot, minced
2 Tbsp. lowfat mayonnaise
1 lime, zest & juice
dash Tabasco sauce

Combine all ingred. & chill. ♥

SOME PEOPLE REGARD DISCIPLINE AS A CHORE.
FOR ME, IT IS A KIND OF ORDER THAT SETS ME
FREE TO FLY. ♥ Julie Andrews

POACHED COD
with tomato gravy

So easy & quick & pure health. Serve this with Garlic Mashed Potatoes (p.95). Put a spoonful of potatoes in a wide shallow bowl, lay the poached cod over the top, surround potatoes with tomato gravy. Sprinkle chives over. *Heaven in a Dish*

154 CALORIES · 3 G. FAT · 28 G. PROTEIN · 6 G. CARBO
305 MG. SODIUM   Serves 6

2 lb. fresh cod
1 tsp. dried oregano
¼ tsp. cayenne
2 tsp. olive oil
1 14 oz. can whole peeled tomatoes
2 cloves garlic, pressed
2 Tbsp. minced fresh chives or parsley

Wash cod & pat dry. Mix together oregano & cayenne & rub all over fish, both sides. Set aside. Put oil into a large skillet, add tomatoes, breaking them up as you go along — & garlic. Bring to simmer. Lay cod on top, cover skillet & cook 4-5 min. till fish is opaque. Sprinkle on chives & serve. ♥

Observe your dog:
if he is fat
you're not getting
enough exercise.

♥ Evan Esar

108

TANTALIZING
TUNA BURGERS

178 CAL · 6 G. FAT · 28 G. PROTEIN · 109 MG. SODIUM
3 G. CARBO · 1 G. FIBER

Serves 4

Clean, low fat, high protein, omega-3 fatty acid rich & delicious. Serve them with Holy Mole (p. 74), icy cold Cucumber Salad (p. 79), & Spicy Mango Salad (p. 82). ♥

1 egg white	1 tbsp. chili puree w/ garlic
juice & zest of 1 lime	1/4 tsp. chili powder
2 tbsp. cilantro	salt & fresh pepper
1 tbsp. Dijon mustard	1 lb. fresh tuna, cubed

Put all ingredients except tuna into processor. Process until totally blended. Add tuna & pulse just enough to blend completely. Make 4 patties & chill at least 1/2 hr. Grill outside, or inside on a hot, oil-sprayed, ridged grill pan (like the one on p. 100), 3 min. per side. Serve. ♥

Give a man a fish & he eats for a day. Teach him how to fish & you get rid of him for the whole weekend. ♥ Zenna Schaffer

HEALTHY QUICK COOK

*Wholesome, soul-satisfying little meals,
rich in nutrients & great flavor.* ♥

SPAGHETTI SQUASH SPAGHETTI

All you need is a spaghetti squash & a jar of good tomato sauce!
Preheat oven to 350°. Pierce squash & place on baking
sheet. Bake 45 min., turn & cook 15 min. more until
shell gives to the touch. Meanwhile heat up the sauce;
you can jazz it up with sliced mushrooms, celery, fresh
basil, crushed garlic, grated carrot, freshly ground black
pepper. Cut squash in half lengthwise—discard seeds. Draw a
fork through pulp to make "spaghetti." Top with tomato sauce &
serve with Parmesan cheese. ♥

COOKED TOMATOES CONTAIN THE CANCER-FIGHTING BETA-CAROTENE LYCOPENE EAT LOTS!

THIS JUST IN FROM THE "I'LL HAVE WHAT SHE'S HAVING" DEPARTMENT:

"It has nothing to do with my work. It's a personal preference."

TEXAS AGRICULTURE DEPT. ASST. COMMISSIONER *Diane Smith*, WHO OVERSEES
THE MARKETING OF BEEF, EXPLAINING WHY SHE HASN'T EATEN MEAT
IN 14 YEARS.

Cheese-Topped ROASTED VEGETABLES With BROWN RICE

It doesn't take much to put together this filling little dinner.
Altho' it's pure "girl food" it's also one of my guy's favorites:
Preheat oven to 350°. For each person put about 1 c.
cooked brown rice in individual oven-proof dishes.
Top each with chopped tomato, minced green onions,
finely chopped broccoli, grated carrot, minced parsley, freshly ground pepper. Grate over a bit of
low-fat mozzarella & a Tbsp. of Parmesan. Bake ½ hr.

1 TBSP. PARMESAN CHEESE HAS ONLY 23 CALORIES & 1.5 FAT GRAMS & BIG FLAVOR

One sits the whole day at the desk and Appetite is standing next to me. "Away with you," I say. But Comrade Appetite does not budge from the spot. ♥ *Leonid Brezhnev*

TOASTED PITA BREAD SANDWICH

Make extra to have ready in the fridge & presto chango, lunch! ♥

Put all kinds of chopped veggies & herbs into a food processor — such as tomatoes, cucumbers, carrots, cabbage, red onion (or chives), parsley, basil; add some walnuts & maybe some low-fat cheese, cooked chicken or tofu; add 1 Tbsp. Dijon mustard to help bind & process to rice-like consistency. Pile into toasted pita bread.

WHOLE WHEAT PITA BREAD IS LOW IN FAT, HIGH IN FIBER & ALSO MAKES GREAT CROUTONS

Fresh Fish & Veggies

The perfect heart-healthy meal in minutes ♥.

Put a piece of skinless salmon, halibut, or cod into a skillet with 1" of water. Add a couple of handfuls of fresh chopped vegetables & herbs, sliced almonds & maybe a sprinkle of red pepper flakes. Cover & steam till almost done (when fish is opaque); add a handful of raw spinach. Cover & cook till fish is just done. Serve with a slotted spoon. Squeeze lemon juice over fish & veggies; cider vinegar over spinach ♥.

SALMON IS ESPECIALLY HIGH IN THE GOOD OMEGA 3 FATTY ACIDS

I PREFER HOSTESS
FRUIT PIES TO
POP-UP TOASTER
TARTS BECAUSE
THEY REQUIRE
LESS COOKING.
♥ Carrie Snow

RISE & SHINE, IT'S BREAKFAST!

If you really want to shine, glow, jump start your day, you need much more than a toaster tart —you need energy!

Make a bowl full of fresh fruit, the juicier the better — choose from watermelon, red grapes, cantaloupe, strawberries — all kinds of berries (loaded with antioxidants ♥); add some plain low-fat yogurt & a sprinkle of good, crunchy granola. Stir. ♥

A jar of plain egg whites will keep forever in the fridge, taste delicious & make wonderful high-protein, low fat & low-calorie omelets. Even better with spinach or broccoli, low-fat cheese, leftover chicken, green onions, mushrooms, & freshly ground pepper. Serve with a half of a Ruby Red grapefruit. ♥

Baked apple! Preheat oven to 350°. Mix together a little oats, brown sugar, walnuts, cinnamon, nutmeg, lemon juice — bind with a little applesauce. Stuff into hollowed-out cavity of a nice big baking apple (Rome Beauty or Cortland). Bake 25 min. ♥

Muesli to serve ☺ One: Put a serving of oats (normal slow-cooking Quaker —uncooked) into a bowl. Sprinkle with cinnamon, raisins, chopped walnuts. Cover with low-fat milk. Stir, cover, & refrigerate 1 hour (or overnight). Delicious as is — or sprinkle with chopped apple.

ENERGY IS MORE ATTRACTIVE THAN BEAUTY...
♥ Louisa May Alcott

Feeling the need for speed?

But you have to eat... try these quick ENERGIZERS to get you off on the right foot:

- ♥ A glass of V-8 juice & a skinless roasted chicken breast
- ♥ Cottage cheese in the cavity of ½ cantaloupe w/chopped peanuts
- ♥ Instead of sugary, store-bought fruited yogurt, add "fruit only" jam to plain yogurt — sprinkle with just a little granola & GO!

MORNING THUNDER

SOY PROTEIN POWDER IS AVAILABLE IN HEALTH FOOD STORES — IT PACKS A PUNCH! READ THE INGRED. ON THE CONTAINER, ADD IT TO YOUR MORNING SMOOTHIE & SAY "WATCH OUT WORLD... HERE I COME." ♥

EACH RECIPE MAKES 2 10 oz. GLASSES

Start your engines please: In a blender put 1 c. orange juice, 1 c. cranberry juice, 6 large fresh or frozen strawberries, ½ c. frozen raspberries, 1 banana, & ¼ c. soy protein powder (& ice, if you like). Blend well. ♥

PER SERVING · 317 CALORIES · 1 G. FAT

Varooom

Into a blender: 1½ c. pear juice, 1 large banana, ¾ c. frozen (or fresh) blueberries, 3 Tbsp. soy protein powder, 1 Tbsp. flax seed oil (so good for you but optional), & 1 c. ice. Blend well. ♥

PER SERVING · 315 CALORIES · 7 G. FAT (from oil)

& one more: Blend 1 c. soymilk, 1 c. o.j., 6 frozen strawberries, 2 Tbsp. sliced almonds, 1 tsp. vanilla, 1 c. ice. 168 CALORIES · 4 G. FAT

Vitality... the one gift that no art could counterfeit. ♥ Storm Jameson

HEALTH FOOD: THE FOOD THEY SERVE IN HELL.

Diet Lite

REMEMBER, YOU'RE ALL ALONE IN THE KITCHEN & NO ONE CAN SEE YOU. ♥ J. Child

THERE ARE NO CALORIES IN CHILDREN'S LEFTOVERS. ♥

CRUMBLE UP YOUR COOKIES. COOKIE CRUMBS HAVE WAY LESS CALORIES THAN WHOLE COOKIES. ♥

IF NO ONE SEES YOU EAT IT, THEN YOU DIDN'T.

DIET COKE CANCELS OUT FRENCH FRIES. ♥

WORKS FOR ME!

GOOD REMEDY FOR FEVER: SNOWCONE

THERE ARE NO CALORIES IN WHAT YOU EAT OFF OF OTHER PEOPLE'S PLATES. ♥

COFFEE WICKS CALORIES AWAY FROM DUNKED DONUTS.

WHAT YOU EAT STANDING UP DOESN'T COUNT. ♥

BIG GULP

ANYBODY THAT TELLS YOU GETTING THIN "TAKES ABOUT A WEEK" IS LYING. ♥ EEYORE (A.A. MILNE)

EAT CARAMELS RATHER THAN CHOCOLATE CREAMS. CALORIES ARE WORKED OFF BY EXTRA CHEWING. ♥

IF YOU WANT TO LOOK YOUNG & THIN HANG OUT WITH OLD FAT PEOPLE. ♥ J. EASON

Sugar and Spice and Everything Nice

Chocolate:

IT'S NOT JUST FOR BREAKFAST ANYMORE ♥

We knew, if we waited long enough, someday they'd tell us that chocolate is a "health" food & TRA-LA ~ the day has come! I was watching Good Morning America this morning & Dr. Joyce Brothers came on with the Good News. She said that chocolate was the number one food choice for American women (we knew that) & here's what else:

- ▲ Moderate chocolate eating makes you live longer! (She said "moderate" is 3 (THREE) candy bars a week!) (GLORY GLORY GLORY)
- ▼ Chocolate is a mood elevator! (YA HOOO)
- ▲ Chocolate has chemicals that mimic the feeling of falling in love ♥♥ (ahhhh).
- ◀ Chocolate doesn't cause acne (yipeeee).
- ▶ Eating chocolate improves memory (& DON'T YOU FORGET IT!) (what?)
- ▲ Chocolate has no cholesterol in it (except for milk chocolate). (THAT'S A BIG 10-4)
- ◀ Chocolate keeps us on an even keel (Ommmmm).
- ▶ Hershey's Chocolate Syrup is fat free. (ZIPPITY DOO-DAH-DAY!)

And last but not least, a piece of candy from a candy box is small enough that no one expects you to share it ♥. (Yay!)

BRITT ATE LOTS OF CHOCOLATE BUT NEVER GOT FAT ~ A SURE SIGN OF DEMONIC POSSESSION. ♥ Erica Jong

♪ TELL ME WHAT YOU WANT
WHAT YOU REALLY REALLY WANT ♪

TRUFFLES

Between two evils, I always pick the one I never tried before.
Mae West ♥

5 oz. good unsweetened chocolate, chopped
2½ c. powdered sugar, sifted
1 stick unsalted butter, room temp.
4 Tbsp. Grand Marnier, rum, or bourbon, opt.
toasted coconut, chopped walnuts, or unsweetened cocoa (sifted),
    for rolling truffles in

Melt chocolate over very low heat in a heavy saucepan. Remove from heat; stir in sugar & butter, a little at a time. Add alcohol & beat well. Roll into little balls & place on waxed paper. Roll in coconut or walnuts, or allow to cool completely then roll in cocoa powder. Serve at room temperature ♥.

CHOCOLATE BRITTLE

You need a candy thermometer   ¼ c. water
        2 c. sugar   10 oz. sliced almonds
    1 lb. unsalted butter   8 oz. good unsweetened chocolate

Combine sugar, butter & water in lg. heavy pot. Stirring constantly, bring to boil over med. high heat. Boil rapidly, stirring, till temp. reaches 295° on thermometer. Remove from heat. Quickly stir in almonds & spread thinly on 2 cookie sheets. Melt choc. over very low heat. When candy is just barely warm, almost cool, brush w/ chocolate. When choc. has dried, break into pieces & store in airtight container. ♥

All the things I really like to do are either immoral, illegal or fattening. ♥ Alexander Woollcott

SET THE MOOD ♥ TRY: LOUIS ARMSTRONG VERVE 823 446-2 ♥ FRANK SINATRA REPRISE 9 26723-2 ♥ ROSEMARY CLOONEY CONCORD JAZZ CCD-4060 ♥ JIMMY DURANTE WARNER BROS. 2-45456 ♥ ELLA & LOUIS VERVE 825374-2 ♥ FRENCH MUSIC/EDITH PIAF DEJA VU 5062-2 ♥ SOUNDTRACKS: SLEEPLESS IN SEATTLE SONY EK 53764 ♥ FRENCH KISS MERCURY 314 528 136-2 ♥

For several days we had to live on nothing but food and water. ♥ W.C. Fields

COCKTAILS

Shine up those darling little glasses you found at the antique store or use martini glasses— just No paper cups please. Fun & festive, these special drinks are guaranteed to jumpstart the conversation ♥. For best results, chill all ingredients.

COSMOPOLITAN

1 PART VODKA
1/2 PART TRIPLE SEC
1/4 PART ROSE'S LIME JUICE
2 PARTS CRANBERRY JUICE

SHAKE WITH ICE & STRAIN INTO A MARTINI GLASS. GARNISH WITH A THIN SLICE OF LIME.

"It was so cold I almost got married."
Shelly Winters

PARISIAN TAXI

TAXI

WATCH OUT FOR HIT AND RUN!
1 PART STOLI VANILLA VODKA
1 PART TIA MARIA
2 PARTS STRONG COFFEE OR ESPRESSO, DECAF OR NOT

CHILL ALL INGRED. SHAKE WITH ICE & STRAIN INTO GLASS RIMMED W/ SUGAR OR CINNAMON-SUGAR. (RIM GLASS W/VODKA & DIP INTO SAUCER FILLED W/SUGAR.) ♥

HULA GIRL

THIS HAS MANY REDEEMING QUALITIES: A BANANA FOR INSTANCE, & JUICE!
PREPARE GLASSES: RUB RIM W/LIME JUICE & DIP INTO COLORED SUGAR. SERVE W/ A PARASOL.
MAKES 1 BLENDER-FULL
3/4 C. RUM
1/2 C. MANGO JUICE
1/2 C. PINEAPPLE JUICE
2 TB. GRAND MARNIER
1 WHOLE RIPE BANANA
FRESH LIME
NUTMEG
PUT 1ST 5 INGRED. IN BLENDER, FILL W/ICE; BLEND WELL. POUR INTO GLASS, W/ A SQUEEZE OF LIME & A SPRINKLE OF NUTMEG. ♥

SWEET LORETTA
Mudslide

1 PART ABSOLUT VODKA
1 PART KAHLUA
1 PART BAILEY'S IRISH CREAM
(1 PART KISS YOUR HINEY GOOD-BYE)
1 SCOOP VANILLA ICE CREAM

PUT EVERYTHING INTO A BLENDER W/LOTS OF ICE. POUR INTO A GLASS RIMMED IN CINNAMON-SUGAR. (RUN WET (KAHLUA) FINGER AROUND RIM OF GLASS & DIP IT IN CINNAMON-SUGAR.)

I'M AS PURE AS THE DRIVEN SLUSH.
Tallulah Bankhead

Wine is proof that God loves us & wants us to be happy. ♥ anon.

(BUT NOT TOO HAPPY)

117

THE SKINNY

EWE'S NOT FAT... JUST FLUFFY ♡

Helpful Hints:

Before you get out of bed in the morning S·T·R·E·T·C·H out like a cat — to give you an awareness of your body.

When you first get up in the morning put your head outside & take a big drink of fresh air to start your day. (I do it just before bedtime too.) Fresh clean air is a very relaxing thing & relieves stress. ♡

Plan what you're going to eat for the day before you get out of bed. Consciousness is your best ally. ♡

When I am bored I sometimes find myself standing in front of the refrigerator peering in as though maybe Julia Child will hand me out a plate of something delicious. Don't let this happen to you! Get out of the house, go for a walk, drink a big glass of water. Stay busy.

Cravings come in waves. If you can just STAND it for a few minutes, they will pass. ♡

My mother said to me, "Honey, listen to that little voice inside you" and I told her, "Oh _Mom_, I ate him a long time ago." ♡ Joanne Rowland

Fad diets cause muscle loss. When you gain the weight back (& all the studies say you WILL) it will be FAT, not muscle. Very low calorie diets _lower_ metabolism. (no good.) ♡

Exercise is the cure. Just 20 minutes of exercise a day can change

More your life — put a wiggle in your walk, a sparkle in your eye & a song in your heart! Exercise raises your metabolism which means you will continue to burn calories even when you're sleeping.

Eat dinner early & keep it small — like a healthy bowl of soup or a big sweet potato. Try not to eat pasta or bread after 2 pm.

If you are in a restaurant & you want dessert but only want a bite — OK, but be ready. Arm yourself — get the salt shaker in one hand, fork in the other — eat your bite. Savor it. OK, eat another bite — now madly salt the rest of it like crazy without thinking about what you are doing. #1 It's your dessert, you have the choice of what to do with it. #2 You

have the POWER over the salt and the dessert. #3 You saved yourself and had dessert! :· IMPRESSIVE!

Pray to God, but continue to row toward shore.
♡ RUSSIAN PROVERB

As you can see from the entry above, all this food anxiety can make you crazy. It's not all about being thin.

PROVERB
A BEAUTIFUL WOMAN WITH A VACANT MIND IS GOOD ONLY FOR FRIGHTENING FISH WHEN SHE FALLS INTO THE WATER. ♡

The real prizes are energy, vitality, self-confidence, strength of spirit, character, & grace. ♡

A SOUND MIND IN A SOUND BODY
Nourish a wholesome discipline but don't be too hard on yourself. Women have traditionally been encouraged to meet unrealistic physical goals (Scarlett O'Hara had a 17" waist!). Don't fall for it — please yourself. ♡

UPPER-BODY EXERCISE

STRENGTH TRAINING MAKES STRONG BONES
(AND MAYBE SOME OF THOSE CUTE LITTLE MUSCLES IN YOUR ARMS)

Remember, the scenery only changes for the lead dog.

S T R E T C H   O U T   T O   W A R M   U P

Slow & Easy Does it. ♥

BICEP CURL

Stand w/feet shoulder-width apart. Hold weights w/palms facing legs. Alternating arms, slowly bring weight to shoulder, then back to starting position.

Weights come 1LB, 3LB, 5LB, ETC. CHALLENGE YOURSELF BUT DON'T HURT YOURSELF.

BEST TO LIFT HEAVIER WEIGHTS & DO LESS REPS THAN LIGHT WEIGHTS & LOTS OF REPS.

♥

Without discipline, there's no life at all.

♥ Katharine Hepburn

A "REP" IS ONE LIFT. 15 REPS IS THE SAME LIFT 15 TIMES, CALLED A "SET."

THERE ARE BOOKS GALORE ON THIS SUBJECT. ♥

SHOULDER PRESS

Stand with feet shoulder-width apart & stomach tight. Hold weights w/palms forward. Start w/ both weights shoulder-height. Slowly extend arms above head then back to starting position.

♪ SHE'S A MANIAC, MANIAC ON THE FLOOR · · · ♪

MOVE DANCE JUMP WALK STRETCH BEND RUN LIFT LEAP... LIVE OUT LOUD

No one can make you feel inferior without your consent. ♥ Eleanor Roosevelt

Regular exercise reduces stress, provides psychological & physical hardiness.

♪ Oh no not I, I will survive... ♪

REST BETWEEN SETS

LATERAL SHOULDER RAISE

Start with weights at sides, palms forward. Slowly raise arms to sides, shoulder level. Lower to starting position.

Theory
FOR QUICKEST FITNESS RESULTS: SHOCK THE BODY BY VARYING ROUTINES. EVERY OTHER DAY, DO YOUR WEIGHTS ~ ON THE OTHER DAYS, ALTERNATE WORKOUTS: BIKE, SWIM, TENNIS, RUN, DANCE, WALK, ETC.

We are the hero of our own story.
♥ Mary McCarthy

THE GOOD NEWS IS THAT YOU CAN GAIN MUSCLE MASS AT ANY AGE ♥. IMPROVE BONE DENSITY & FIGHT OSTEOPOROSIS.

THE ONLY WAY TO IT IS THROUGH IT.
♥ Joan Fisher Dat

THERE'S NOTHIN' TO IT. YOU JUST DO IT. ♥

The Prayer Pose: My friend taught me this yoga position years ago. She said it

promoted relaxation ~ I love the stretch. Breathe deeply & remain in position a few minutes. ♥

IF YOU LIKE THE WAY THIS FEELS, TAKE A YOGA CLASS!

BUTTONS and BOWS

Half the reason we look so good when we've lost weight is because we feel so good — & that confidence shows. We dress better, stand taller, get a new hairdo, try a new lipstick & smile more. So it may not be as much about being thin as it is about self-confidence. ♥ Many wonderful gifts were given to women, of them we are quite aware ♥. One of them is that WE are the ones who get to wear the cute stuff — & we don't have to be 110 lbs. to do it! So tie a ribbon in your hair, paint your toenails Kiss Me Pink, get some new sunglasses & show 'em what you're made of (sugar, spice, nice, etc.). Charm is in the details.

As LIZA MINNELLI SAYS: "Reality is something You rise above."

TIE BRACELETS TOGETHER WITH A SATIN RIBBON. ♥

SMELL GOOD

N°5 CHANEL PERFUME

STYLIN' SUNGLASSES

BAGS, CLUTCHES, & CUTE LITTLE PURSES

HATS

DO YOUR PART TO MAKE THIS WORLD A CUTER PLACE TO LIVE IN. ♥

To Us

Well, that's all for now ~ I'm glad to be done, but sad to go! Like all endings, this is just the beginning ~ here we are starting a whole new century (millennium!) together. All that is past is herstory & the future is ours to dream. GIRLFRIENDS FOREVER

FARE THEE WELL, AND

May the road rise up to meet you.
May the wind be always at your back,
the sun shine warm upon your face,
the rain fall soft upon your fields,
and until we meet again
May God hold you in the hollow of Her hand.

Byelle

LIFE IS GOOD

WHEN I WAS ABOUT TWENTY-TWO, LONG BEFORE I HAD PAINTED MY FIRST PICTURE, I HAD A DREAM THAT I HAD A KNITTING AND EMBROIDERY SHOP AND ALL DAY LONG ALL MY GIRLFRIENDS CAME TO THE STORE AND WE MADE THINGS AND TALKED AND DRANK TEA~ MY DREAM HAS COME TRUE~ EXCEPT IT ISN'T A KNITTING STORE, BUT MORE LIKE A CREATIVE COUNTRY STORE. AND ALL MY GIRLFRIENDS COME OVER AND WE TEST RECIPES AND TASTE AND TALK AND DRINK TEA WHILE I PAINT. WE DO CHOCOLATE "TASTE TESTS" EVERY DAY. THERE IS A WONDERFUL HAPPY ENERGY IN THE HOUSE. I WANT TO THANK THESE GOOD FRIENDS WHO HELPED ME WITH RECIPES, KEPT US LAUGHING, KEPT THIS HOUSE GOING, AND GAVE UNENDING SUPPORT. ♥ TO SHELLY STEWART, SARAH SERGI, ANNA LOWELL (LOWLY), DENISE COGLIANO, TINA MILLER, MARGOT DATZ, EDITE KROLL, MARCELLE BEN DAVID, NOREEN FLANDERS, AND CINDY PETROP. AND TO MY M♥M AND D♥D WHO ALWAYS KEEP ME ENTERTAINED ON THE PHONE. AND ALL OF MY DEAR-EST BEST FRIENDS WHO ARE SO OBVIOUSLY MY INSPIRATION. THANKS FOR THE MEMORIES ♥. BUT MOST OF ALL, I WANT TO THANK MY VERY BEST FRIEND OF ALL, WHO'S NOT EVEN A GIRLFRIEND, BUT MY ALL-AMERICAN GUY JOE B. HALL MAN OF MY DREAMS, LOVE OF MY LIFE, GUARDIAN ANGEL EXTRAORDINAIRE, WHO LIKES ME JUST THE WAY I AM · ♥

HEARTS CAN INSPIRE OTHER HEARTS WITH THEIR FIRE

Special Thanks to Little, Brown & Company for Years of support & especially to my editor, Mary Tondorf-Dick ♥.

My gift is my song, this song's for you.

Elton John

and me too ♪ . . .

Send me your name & address & I'll put you on my mailing list: ♥ Susan Branch, Box 2463, Vineyard Haven, MA 02568 ~ or just say Hi ♥

WE WENT SHOPPING · WE KEPT SECRETS · WE PLAYED HOPSCOTCH · WE LAY IN THE SUN · WE WENT DANCING · WE HAD TEA · WE WORE MINI SKIRTS · WE SANG IN THE CAR · WE ATE FRENCH FRIES · WE BORROWED CLOTHES · WE CRUISED FOR GUYS · WE WENT TO LUNCH · WE TRIED ON HATS · WE WENT TO PARIS · WE LIP SYNCED · WE LAUGHED SOOOOO HARD ·